Praise for *I'm Waiting, God*

Barb Roose tackles the topic of patience in a way that really hit home for me personally. I have a lot of "why, how, and when" questions for God. Combining in-depth Scripture study with practical tools and personal stories, this study is one of the best I've ever read!

—**Melissa Spoelstra**, Bible teacher, speaker, and author of *Romans: Good News That Changes Everything* and numerous other Bible studies and books

When waiting is hard and long, the last thing you need is someone disregarding your pain, with platitudes like "just push through." In I'm Waiting, God, Barb walks with us in our waiting. Warm, tender, and a help for moving forward, Barb's study has left me stronger, knowing I can wait so His glory is seen.

—**Lynn Cowell**, author of *Make Your Move* and member of the Proverbs 31 Ministries speaker and writer team

Barb Roose is a wonderful role model of walking out biblical truth while in life's waiting room. This study is a must read for anyone wondering what to do while waiting and wanting to stay close to God in the meantime.

—**Pam Farrel**, best-selling author of over forty books, including *Discovering Hope in the Psalms: A Creative Bible Study Experience*

This study will help you trust God even when His timing doesn't make sense. Barb tenderly guides you through God's Word and her own personal examples of God's faithfulness, assuring you that you aren't alone as you wait for God to move. You'll find peace about God's provision and a deeper understanding of God's desire to take care of you.

—**Heather M. Dixon**, speaker and author of *Determined: Living Like Jesus in Every Moment*

If anyone has the authority to write this book, Barb does. I have watched her exude joy and relentless gratitude for life and living through her own unexpected delay. The hope she offers comes from her resolve to find and celebrate God's abundant blessing in spite of difficult delays.

—**Kia Stephens**, writer, creator of *The Father Swap* blog, and founder of Entrusted Women

A FOUR-WEEK BIBLE STUDY

BARB ROOSE

I'm Waiting, God

FINDING BLESSING
IN GOD'S DELAYS

Abingdon Women/Nashville

I'm Waiting, God
Finding Blessing in God's Delays

ISBN 978-1-5018-8862-5

19 20 21 22 23 24 25 26 27 28 — 10 9 8 7 6 5 4 3 2 1
MANUFACTURED IN THE UNITED STATES OF AMERICA

Contents

About the Author 6

Introduction 7

Week 1: Hannah: From Waiting to Worshiping (1 Samuel 1) 12
    Group Session Guide 38

Week 2: Ruth: God, Now What? (Ruth 1-4) 42
    Group Session Guide 70

Week 3: The Unnamed Bleeding Woman: Healing from the
    Inside Out (Mark 5:24-34) 74
    Group Session Guide 102

Week 4: Martha: Embracing the Better Blessing (John 11) 108
    Group Session Guide 137

Self-Study Verse Bank 142

Leader Helps 148

Notes 155

About the Author

Barb Roose is a popular speaker and author who is passionate about connecting women to one another and to God, helping them apply the truths of God's Word to the practical realities and challenges they face as women in today's culture. Barb enjoys teaching and encouraging women at conferences and events across the country, as well as internationally. She is the author of the *Joshua: Winning the Worry Battle* and *Beautiful Already: Reclaiming God's Perspective on Beauty* Bible studies and the books *Winning the Worry Battle: Life Lessons from the Book of Joshua* and *Enough Already: Winning Your Ugly Struggle with Beauty*. She also writes a regular blog at BarbRoose.com and hosts the "Better Together" podcast. Previously, Barb was executive director of Ministry at CedarCreek Church in Perrysburg, Ohio, where she served on staff for fourteen years and co-led the annual Fabulous Women's Conference that reached more than ten thousand women over five years. Barb lives with her family in Toledo, Ohio.

Follow Barb:

 @barbroose

 @barbroose

 Facebook.com/barbararoose

Blog   BarbRoose.com (check here for event dates and booking information)

Introduction

Have you ever prayed, "God, please give me more patience!" Who hasn't uttered that desperate prayer in a difficult situation? In our day, speed rules. We live in a world where webpages load in an instant, a frozen roast can cook in thirty minutes, and online orders deliver next day. Waiting seems ridiculous if there's a way to get something fast. Of course, we expect God to move fast as well; and when He doesn't, it frustrates us.

Have you ever found yourself in need of a breakthrough, a redo, or a rescue? When something in our lives is missing, broken, or changed, we hit our knees and cry out to God to grant us the good thing that we want. However, when that prayer goes unanswered, we might start asking some uncomfortable questions. Does God care? Does He love me? Can I keep living like this? What if God doesn't give me what I'm asking? Even if you know that God can answer your prayer, you may wonder if He will before you run out of time.

Waiting on God challenges our faith, doesn't it?

As a Christ-follower, I love Jesus with all my heart, but that doesn't mean that patience comes easy to me. Even now, my heart bears the Jesus-healed scars of the impatient seasons when I tried to fix people, force solutions, or manipulate my personal feelings to avoid the fear that comes in the face of losing control. In those days, my problem was that I prayed for God to move, but I didn't have the faith to wait. Sitting in the "waiting room" of life is never easy.

Many years ago, an addiction crisis emerged in our home. At first, I tried to fix it. I failed. Then I prayed for God to make it go away. That went unanswered. So I prayed harder. The situation grew worse. Was God angry with me? Why wasn't He answering my prayer? I wrestled with God, begging Him to end our struggle and heal my suffering.

In the midst of that unanswered prayer, I discovered God's better blessing for my life. When I stopped panicking and started focusing on being in His presence,

God filled the parts of my heart broken by pain and suffering with what I needed most, which was more of Him. Even though my waiting years began with worry and wrestling, a number of years ago I finally settled into the place God has intended for me all along: worship. Experiencing the presence of God is greater than the good things that I prayed for, and that has been the best blessing of my life.

What about you? How are you handling the unanswered prayers in your life? On a scale of 1-10, how much do you struggle to be patient? Don't beat yourself up if you lose patience quickly with others or God. There is no easy-button solution for learning how to wait for God's timing. This journey looks more like a winding path instead of a formulaic three-step plan. Here's the unique twist: your path to patience is paved right over the road of your unanswered prayers.

So, if you're tired of losing your temper or making rash decisions when you're fed up and can't take any more, you might be ready to discover the blessings that God has for you in a season of waiting.

During this study you'll meet four women in the Bible who grappled with unanswered prayers:

1. One woman wondered if God loved her or had forgotten about her. (Hannah)
2. One woman's life took a tragic and unexpected turn. (Ruth)
3. One woman suffered for over a decade with an embarrassing medical condition. (the unnamed bleeding woman)
4. One woman prayed, but God said "no" to her prayer. (Martha)

Perhaps you relate to one or more of their stories. These ancient women didn't have perfect faith, and at times they even offered angry, desperate prayers. So, if you're feeling anxious, angry, discouraged, or depressed because God hasn't answered your prayers, their stories will breathe fresh hope and practical next steps into your life. Together we'll discover that there are many blessings just waiting to be discovered during times of waiting, including a closer relationship with God than we've ever dared to dream.

Getting Started

Over the next four weeks we will dig into the lives of these four women—Hannah, Ruth, the unnamed bleeding woman, and Martha—who all endured a long season of sadness, pain, and unanswered prayer. Yet our focus won't be on the beginning or end of their stories; rather, we'll dive deep into the lessons and blessings they teach us about how we can develop the faith to wait on God when our prayers are not being answered according to our timeline or agenda.

Your Personal Study

The study has been designed with a flexible format to fit most any season of life. Each week offers three days of Bible study homework, plus two optional days for more personal reflection to be enjoyed as time or energy permits:

Days 1-3
- Dig into the Scripture and explore a specific Waiting Room Problem (Day 1), a Waiting Room Principle (Day 2), and a Waiting Room Application (Day 3).

Days 4 and 5 (*Optional*)
- Enjoy a Scripture Self-Study.
- Wrap up the week with a devotional reading and a prayer journaling exercise.

Each day includes a Daily Gratitude exercise, and Days 1-3 include a summary of the main idea called Today's Takeaway. You'll also find a Memory Verse Reflection on Day 1 and a Wrap-Up for the Bible Study lessons on Day 3. These features plus the many practical exercises sprinkled throughout will give you the tools you need to put the concepts we're studying into practice in your own life.

In addition to this workbook, all you need is a Bible or access to an online Bible app and a pen. The lessons for Days 1-3 will take approximately 20-30 minutes to complete. If you choose to do the Scripture Self-Study on Day 4, you can determine how much time to spend according to how in-depth you'd like to go. And if you choose to do the devotional reading and prayer journaling exercise on Day 5, you'll want to allow about 10-15 minutes (though you can choose to spend more time journaling if you desire).

Meeting with a Group

When studying with a group, you'll gather each week to watch a video, discuss what you're learning, and pray together. The session outlines, which provide options for both a 60-minute and a 90-minute session, include discussion questions, activities, prayer prompts, and notes for the video segment. You'll find the outline for each session at the end of the personal lessons for that week.

If you're the facilitator or leader of your group, you'll want to check out the additional leader helps at the back of this book. Ideally group members should complete the first week of lessons before your first group session. This is because each video message complements the content that you have studied during the week. However, feel free to adapt the study as you wish to meet the needs of your particular group. Whether or not your group watches the video, the questions and activities will guide you in sharing your experiences and learnings together.

Bonus!

If you'd like additional encouragement, you can sign up for "The Patience Path," a 30-day email devotional that I've created to go along with the study. To sign up, go to barbroose.com/patiencepath.

Before You Begin

If you're wondering whether this four-week study will be as fruitful as a longer study, the answer is yes! It is my hope that you will find the flexible format both inviting and practical for your busy life, helping you to be more successful in completing the material. As a result, you should experience just as much spiritual growth—and possibly even more—in these four weeks as you would in a longer, more involved study.

I want you to know that I've been praying over this content and those who will encounter it—and that includes you. I'm believing that God knows exactly what you're facing and that He has a special blessing planned for you in the next four weeks and beyond. God desires to equip you with everything you need to trust His promises and wait for His divine timing in your life. Though our life stories are different, I know the frustration of unanswered prayer and the fear that time will run out. Yet God can be trusted as we hang out in the "waiting room" of life. And best of all, He blesses us even in the midst of the delay!

This verse remains fixed in my heart, and it is my prayer for you:

> *"Be still, and know that I am God."*
> (Psalm 46:10)

I don't know your unanswered prayer, but I do know God is faithful. I am trusting that He will be working in your heart, mind, and life over the next four weeks. You are not alone in this journey; and most of all, God will not let you down but will satisfy your deepest need.

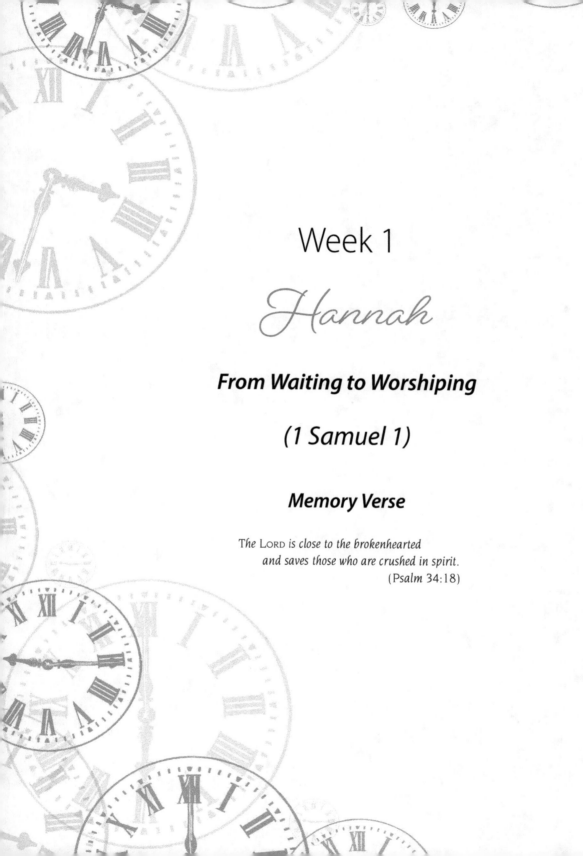

Week 1

Hannah

From Waiting to Worshiping

(1 Samuel 1)

Memory Verse

The LORD is close to the brokenhearted
and saves those who are crushed in spirit.
(Psalm 34:18)

Have you ever sat in a hospital waiting room while a loved one had surgery, delivered a baby, or underwent a biopsy? There are many ways we try to keep ourselves busy while we're waiting. We sit. We stand. We pace. We drink old coffee and flip through even older magazines.

I've spent long hours, even some overnights, in hospital waiting rooms. I remember the long hours I waited during a friend's organ transplant and another time when I anxiously awaited the outcome of a family member's delicate heart surgery. While pacing or flipping through magazines, I would attempt to pray a few words every couple of hours. The rest of the time, I would stare off into space as I struggled with feeling helpless and worrying about how things might turn out. Waiting rooms tended to bring to the surface difficult questions and feelings about God that I'd rather have kept buried deep inside.

It has taken a long time for me to learn the following: In the space between what I'm waiting for and the actual outcome, God is working just as much in my heart as He is in my situation. This means that for me—and for you—that waiting room time doesn't have to be wasted time! If you're in a situation today where you've been praying and pacing but nothing has seemed to change, don't lose hope! If you are following God, He is at work in you as much as He is at work in your circumstances.

In this week's study, you'll learn from Hannah, a woman who prayed many years of unanswered prayers. In the space between what she was praying for and the eventual outcome, Hannah felt that God had forgotten her. What's more, the people around her either minimized her pain or bullied her into even greater sadness. This week Hannah will teach you to become a bold woman of faith, even if you must continue to hang out in your "waiting room" for the foreseeable future.

If you know Hannah's story, you know that God did eventually honor her prayer. However, the point of learning Hannah's story isn't that God gave her what she wanted; it's that Hannah found the blessing in bravely and boldly turning toward God. As she prayed, Hannah's faith revealed her desire to worship God rather than continue to suffer in her waiting.

Day 1: God Is Closer Than You Think

WAITING ROOM PROBLEM

When your prayers are unanswered, do you feel like God has forgotten you or doesn't love you?

Has it ever seemed that God is answering everyone else's prayers but yours? If you're waiting on God to send a significant other, your social media newsfeed is flooded with happy couples. If you're waiting on a baby, pregnancy announcements fill your mailbox. Waiting on your body to heal? You notice the easy, carefree bounce in everyone else's step. It's pretty frustrating when the view from your "waiting room" is filled with people getting the very things that you want. You sigh and, if you're still talking to God, whisper, "I'm waiting, God. What about me?"

As we look at Hannah's story this week, her waiting room of infertility is a powerful symbol and painful reality of waiting. A baby is a tangible symbol of a good thing in life. So, when you pray and God doesn't give you that good thing, whatever it might be, your unanswered prayer might spark unsettling questions about your self-worth and God's sovereignty or goodness.

Infertility isn't the only tender waiting room in life. No matter "where" you're waiting for God to answer your prayer, I trust that God will use Hannah's story to illuminate the path to the blessing that He has waiting for you today.

Read 1 Samuel 1:1-2, and answer the questions below.

Who is the man introduced in the story?

Who are the two women mentioned, and what relationship do they have with him?

What information are you given about each of the two women?

Extra Insights

"The Bible presents monogamy as the divine ideal....Apparently, polygamy, like divorce, was tolerated because of the hardness of people's hearts (Matt. 19:8)."[1]

Shiloh was the first permanent home of the tabernacle after Joshua and the Israelites conquered Canaan. The city was the main place of worship for the Israelites until well into Hannah's son, Samuel's years as a prophet.[2]

Since Hannah is mentioned first before Peninnah, she is likely Elkanah's first wife. I've included an Extra Insight in the margin about polygamy in case you might be wondering if God ever condoned men having multiple wives. The quick answer is no. However, Elkanah likely married Peninnah once it was clear that Hannah was unable to have children. When Peninnah began having children, everyone knew that the problem was with Hannah, not her husband. Since the only information we're given about these women is their fertility scorecard, that is a clue to how their culture valued women. It's easy to imagine that Hannah prayed with fervor because her worth and value depended on it.

Now, let's enter into the story. Once a year Elkanah takes his family to Shiloh for a special time of offering sacrifices and worship. Israelites from all over Canaan would make this trip. Consider this experience from Hannah's perspective. Inevitably, Hannah would run into other women who had given birth since the previous year, and she would be reminded that another year has passed and her prayers have remained unanswered.

The Land of CANAAN (The Promised Land)

After Elkanah had made the sacrifices for his family, they would sit down to a special meal. It is then that Elkanah gives out portions of meat to his wives and children.

Read 1 Samuel 1:4-5. How much does Elkanah give to Hannah versus Peninnah and her children?

It's here we see Elkanah's love for Hannah. Though he cannot give her what she wants most, he makes this one grand gesture in front of everyone. His action proclaims that he loves and values Hannah even though she is unable to have children.

While Elkanah does his best to show love to his wife, not everyone in the family is supportive.

Read 1 Samuel 1:6-7. How does Peninnah treat Hannah on their annual trip?

Each year, Hannah is so upset by Peninnah's behavior that she is unable to enjoy Elkanah's annual gift. What is Hannah unable to do?

One translation says that Peninnah would "make fun of her mercilessly" (1 Samuel 1:6 CEB). Can you see yourself in Hannah's position? Not only are you not getting what you want; the woman who has what you're dreaming about is bullying you. Talk about rubbing salt into a bleeding wound! Sadly, this scenario happens year after year.

We don't know why Peninnah resorts to such petty behavior every year. Perhaps Peninnah is waiting for any sign that Elkanah could love her as he loves Hannah. Regardless of why Peninnah behaves so meanly toward Hannah, the pain is so great that Hannah never enjoys her double portion. It is an expression of love that is crushed by another's awful behavior.

It seems that Elkanah is aware of Hannah's sadness as well as Peninnah's pettiness. So, he attempts to reframe Hannah's perspective. The only problem is that Elkanah is asking Hannah to look at her situation through his eyes, not hers.

In verse 8, we see that Elkanah asks Hannah why she is so upset. He thinks he is worth more to Hannah than what?

Bless Elkanah's heart, right? While he tries to ease Hannah's pain, his question is like fingernails screeching down the blackboard of her hurting heart. Even though Hannah loves her husband, that doesn't mean she can forget the incredible ache in her heart because the dream of a baby in her arms is unfulfilled.

So many of us can relate to Hannah, right? Think about your life and the other women in your Bible study group or church who show up carrying the burden of unanswered prayers each week. Are you like Hannah, trying to pretend that everything is fine while you're dying inside? Maybe you're showing up at church each week with a pasted-on smile, painfully attempting to worship. But the beat of your broken heart doesn't thump with the rhythm of the music, only with the constant question "God, where are you?"

What have you been praying for that hasn't happened yet?

Circle the emotions that you are currently feeling as you're sitting in the waiting room of an unanswered prayer:

Unloved   Abandoned   Forgotten   Positive

Angry/Frustrated   Upset   Confused   Hopeful

Helpless   Anxious   Numb   Challenged

Other: _____

In one particular waiting season long ago, I prayed for several years that God would provide a full-time position for me at my local church. I worked part-time for a number of years and hoped to transition to full-time work when my youngest daughter began kindergarten. However, the Great Recession then crippled our regional auto-industry economy. As jobs were lost, our church's weekly giving declined. That much-prayed-for full-time position was put on hold indefinitely. Every time I had to squeeze our family budget or say no to a fun opportunity, I'd bluster in prayer, "I'm waiting, God." Back then I would have circled words such as angry, confused, anxious, and helpless.

Why does God sometimes delay answering our prayers? The Bible reveals a number of reasons. Sometimes, God might not answer because of our unforgiveness, secret sin, pride, or wrong motives (see Psalm 66:18, Isaiah 59:1-2, James 1:5-8). But there are other times when God holds off on answering prayer for other reasons.

Word Bank

avoid harm

supernatural
opposition

God's works/
power on display

perseverance
in prayer

⁹"Remember the
former things, those
of long ago;
    I am God, and
    there is no other;
    I am God, and
    there is none
    like me.
¹⁰I make known
the end from the
beginning,
    from ancient times,
    what is still
    to come.
I say, 'My purpose
will stand,
    and I will do all
    that I please.'"
        (Isaiah 46:9-10)

───────────

³⁸ I am convinced
that neither death
nor life, neither
angels nor demons,
neither the present
nor the future, nor
any powers, ³⁹neither
height nor depth, nor
anything else in all
creation, will be able
to separate us from
the love of God that
is in Christ Jesus our
Lord.
        (Romans 8:38-39)

Read the following Scriptures, and summarize the reason for unanswered prayer by filling in the blank using the Word Bank in the margin.

John 9:3

_____

Daniel 10:13

_____

Luke 18:1

_____

Isaiah 55:8-9

_____

As you can see, there are various reasons that the answers to your prayers might be delayed, and some of those reasons have nothing to do with you. Holding on to a healthy perspective when experiencing God's delay is crucial to not missing a blessing that God wants you to experience.

Whenever I feel like God has forgotten me, the most important thing that I can do is to keep a healthy perspective. There are three healthy perspectives that I've learned to hold on to in the face of unanswered prayer.

1. A healthy perspective remembers God's character.

Read Isaiah 46:9-10 in the margin. What do these verses tell you about how God thinks in comparison to how we think?

2. A healthy perspective remembers God's attitude toward you.

Read Romans 8:38-39 in the margin. What can stop God from loving you?

How would you describe God's attitude toward you based on these verses?

3. A healthy perspective remembers God's promises.

Read Jeremiah 29:11 in the margin. What kind of plans does God have for your life? What is your participation in God's plans?

"I know the plans I have for you," declares the LORD, "plans to prosper you and not to harm you, plans to give you hope and a future.

(Jeremiah 29:11)

From our human perspective, God's delay in answering our prayers isn't going to make sense because we can't see everything that God is doing. But we can be sure that God isn't wasting our time while we're in the "waiting room"!

Memory Verse Reflection

At the end of the first lesson each week, you will have an opportunity to reflect on your memory verse. I have selected verses that not only will encourage you during your waiting journey but also will connect you to God's heart and character. You can trust God while you wait!

This week Hannah's story paints a wonderful backdrop to our memory verse, which was penned by a man named David while he was on the run from King Saul. Saul made many attempts to kill David in order to prevent him from becoming king. In fact, David spent fifteen years on the run before he finally became king. At the point when he wrote Psalm 34, David encountered Philistine King Achish of Gath, who wasn't much friendlier than King Saul. So David pretended to be insane so that Achish would let him go (1 Samuel 21:10-15).

While David wrote these words praising God for deliverance, he was a man who understood the fears and frustrations of waiting on God, who often seemed to take His time answering prayer.

Read Psalm 34:18 below, and underline the words that are meaningful or speak to you:

The LORD is close to the brokenhearted
*   and saves those who are crushed in spirit.*

(Psalm 34:18)

How does this verse apply to what you might be facing today?

Many times in life I have clung to Psalm 34:18, even when I wasn't sure that I felt God's presence. I just kept telling myself that He was there whether I could feel Him or not. Let me give that same encouragement to you. Even if you feel that God is far away, I assure you that He is right there with you. And if you are wondering, If God is here with me, why isn't He doing more? the next verse offers some wisdom.

Read Psalm 34:19 in the margin. Even if you don't understand what God is doing in your "waiting room" journey, what is the promise in this verse for those who trust in God?

The righteous person faces many troubles, but the LORD comes to the rescue each time.
(Psalm 34:19 NLT)

Tomorrow you're going to sit with Hannah as she lays the broken pieces of her heart before God in prayer. This isn't a polite or reserved occasion. Hannah gets real and raw about how she feels and makes no apologies. If you've ever felt afraid to be honest before God or struggled to pray because you don't think God cares about you, tomorrow's study will be an eye-opening experience. For us, Hannah's prayer is a powerful demonstration of going boldly before God's throne of mercy (Hebrews 4:16)—and then asking for what we want.

Today's Takeaway

God will never stop loving you, nor will He ever forget about you.

Prayer

God, there are times when I feel that I am forgotten and alone like Hannah. Yet I choose to cling to the words in Psalm 34:18, believing that You are close to me in my "waiting room" times. God, I believe that You will never forget about me and that Your love will never leave me. Please keep whispering those reminders to me today. Amen.

Day 2: The Power of Prayer

WAITING ROOM PRINCIPLE

Prayer is a powerful form of worship that communicates, "I trust You, God."

During long waiting room seasons of my life, I have been challenged to reevaluate my relationship with God and my expectations in prayer.

As a child, prayer was simple because my needs in life were simple. My mom taught me to pray before meals and to thank God for my food. I prayed beside my bed at night and thanked God for my home and family. However, prayer changed for me once I began creating expectations about what I thought my life should look or feel like. Most of my expectations could be summed up in the pursuit of what I defined as the good life. My picture of the good life looked like graduating from college, getting married, having a family, buying a house, getting a well-paying job, and so forth. Since the Bible didn't define any of those things as sins, I figured that if I prayed for those good things, then God would happily give them to me. As those symbols of a good life dropped into my life, I expected that God would sign on to my maintenance plan. If something or someone got a little broken, I dropped to my knees and asked God to fix it.

However, in those waiting room experiences, there have been months and years when I prayed for God to fix something that He previously had blessed, but nothing happened. In those times of life, I often peeled back the layers of my expectations around prayer. Long seasons of painful waiting prompted hard questions such as, Am I doing it wrong? and Does praying even matter if God's going to do what He's going to do? If you've ever asked either of those questions, you aren't alone.

In today's study, Hannah gives us a big, bold example of how to use prayer as a powerful act of worship for connecting with God. Though she might make you nervous with her boldness, she also might inspire you to believe God for bigger and more. God is capable of the impossible, and perhaps He's waiting for you to trust Him for it.

Read 1 Samuel 1:9-10. How is Hannah described as praying?

One commentator observes that the phrase describing the state of Hannah's emotions could be translated as "bitter of soul,"[4] which includes the same word used to describe the attitude of Ruth's mother-in-law, Naomi, toward God and life (Ruth 1:20). We'll explore Ruth's story next week. For now, take a moment and envision what it looked like for Hannah to enter the tabernacle, which would be like you walking into church.

Since Hannah is crying bitterly, I envision a woman whose facial features are twisted in emotional and physical pain because of her circumstance. Perhaps she clutches at a fully saturated piece of fabric, no longer able to wipe away more tears.

Despite her distraught condition, however, Hannah demonstrates great courage by boldly coming to God in prayer. Hannah isn't concerned that others might think she is unhinged and whisper behind her back. She has come to talk with God, and she doesn't care what others think. She prays out of every emotion and ounce of faith that is in her heart.

At first, we don't know what Hannah is saying during her prayer. We just read that she is crying bitterly before God. But then, there is a shift. Some of the words of Hannah's prayer are recorded for us. If you grew up thinking that prayer was a nice, quiet, polite conversation with God, Hannah's prayer is about to surprise you.

Read the following Scripture. Underline the phrase "Lord of heavenly forces," and circle the phrase "remember me."

Then she made this promise: "LORD of heavenly forces, just look at your servant's pain and remember me! Don't forget your servant! Give her a boy! Then I'll give him to the LORD for his entire life. No razor will ever touch his head."

(1 Samuel 1:11 CEB)

Even though we don't know every word that Hannah prayed, what we have here is so powerful. Hannah is calling on God, and she is showing up boldly. First, Hannah addresses God in a way that recognizes how she sees Him, as her protector.[6] Then, Hannah cries out for God to remember her. No doubt she has stacked mountains of prayers up to heaven, yet those prayers have gone unanswered. So, she reminds God who she is. Then she makes her next request: Give me a boy! Talk about keeping it straightforward and simple! I admire her boldness.

What is so powerful to me about this portion of Hannah's prayer is that once she makes her bold request, she surrenders her son back to God in the very next sentence. There are two significant things to notice about Hannah's vow to give her son back to God.

Fill in the blanks by looking back at 1 Samuel 1:11:

1. Hannah vows to give the boy to God for his

_____ life.

2. No _____ will touch his head.

As Hannah keeps praying, we read that someone is watching her, namely Eli, the priest. He noticed Hannah as she entered the tabernacle, and it seems that he is troubled by what he sees.

Read Samuel 1:12-14. What accusation does Eli make?

While Hannah pours out her heart before God in faith, Eli jumps to conclusions, accuses her of being drunk, and tells her to sober up. When I read this, my heart hurts for Hannah in this moment because sometimes we can be accused of all sorts of crazy things when we're acting in faith.

What is Hannah's response to Eli's criticism?

Hannah's name means "woman of grace,"[8] and this is a wonderful example of how beautifully a name fits someone. She doesn't take her distressed feelings out on Eli. She responds versus reacts. Rather than getting defensive or angry, Hannah responds to Eli without returning angry words; she just offers the simple truth. There's a wonderful lesson in this for all of us. During our waiting room experiences, people may misunderstand our struggle or they may misinterpret our motives; and getting mad at them doesn't help our hurt!

Due to a family crisis awhile back, I had to follow through on a decision that I'd begged God to intervene in so that I wouldn't need to make it. In the days that followed, I could barely see through my tears. However, each morning I pulled on my tennis shoes and walked for miles while pouring my heart out to God and listening to worship music. I'm sure that I looked a lot like Hannah did when she entered the tabernacle. Anyone looking out their front window would have seen a tall, disheveled woman wearing sunglasses and holding limp tissues in her hands.

While my actions may have seemed confusing to some, I had complete clarity on what I needed to do: worship God. One of my favorite mental health slogans is "what other people think of me is none of my business." If you are walking by faith during a waiting room season and pouring your heart out to God but others don't get it, you don't have to

Extra Insights

Usually, Levite men served from the time they turned thirty years old to fifty years old (Numbers 4:3). However, Hannah promises God that her son will serve for his entire life, which means that she would turn him over to the high priest once the little boy was weaned.

Any Jewish person could make a nazirite vow, which means not participating in certain activities like haircuts or drinking alcohol. Normally, the nazirite vow is for a period of time, usually counted in days or months (Numbers 6). In the Bible only a few people had a lifetime vow: Samson, Samuel, and John the Baptist. Their nazirite vow was made by their parents before the men were born.[7]

Extra Insight

A person's wisdom yields patience; it is to one's glory to overlook an offense.
(Proverbs 19:11)

get angry or make apologies. Like Hannah, graciously inform them of your actions and then keep worshiping God whether others agree with how you're doing it or not.

Since Hannah's explanation was given with grace and gentleness, Eli's attitude toward her shifted.

How does Eli respond to Hannah in 1 Samuel 1:17?

Not only does this spiritual leader bless Hannah with words of peace, which is the Hebrew word *shalom*,[9] meaning completeness (or wholeness), but he also prays that God will grant her request.

As Hannah leaves the tabernacle, she leaves with an experience she has had for the first time ever since making that annual trip to Shiloh. After pouring her heart out to God in prayer, she has received words of encouragement for her condition and a blessing.

Read 1 Samuel 1:18. What effect does this experience have on Hannah's physical body and emotional state?

Consider Hannah's interactions with Peninnah and her interaction with Eli. While Peninnah is a woman who should understand the pain and anguish of not being able to bear a child, she chooses to bully Hannah into misery. Eli is a man who isn't Hannah's husband, yet he offers her more compassion than Elkanah, who deeply loves his wife. This demonstrates that people don't have to walk in our shoes in order to walk beside us with empathy.

How comfortable or uncomfortable are you telling God what's really on your heart and mind, even if you're upset with Him?

Your view of God determines how you might approach or shy away from Him in prayer. If you think that God is just waiting for you to make a mistake or that He's disappointed in you, then you may feel afraid. If you grew up in a religious tradition where only certain people could come to God, then you'll feel uncomfortable approaching God in an authentic way like Hannah did.

Read Hebrews 4:16 in the margin.

How are you instructed to come to God?

Let us come boldly to the throne of our gracious God. There we will receive his mercy, and we will find grace to help us when we need it most.

(Hebrews 4:16 NLT)

What promise are you given?

Who sits on thrones? Rulers sit on thrones, and not everyone can come rushing in whenever he or she wants. However, as a child of God, you are not only invited to come before God; you're told in advance that you will receive grace and mercy as help when you need it most.

I want to give you permission to bare your soul before God, who isn't just Almighty but also is your Abba Father. He loves and cares for you right now.

Below is a template for you to fill in your bold prayer. Be like Hannah, and don't hold back!

Prayer

Dear God, as Hannah prayed, You are the Lord of Heavenly Armies, the God in charge of the universe. You know me by name, and I know that Your love for me is real and true. Thank You for Hannah's example of authentic prayer, abundant grace, and overflowing faith.

Today I want to pour my heart out to You about _____.

God, I feel so _____.

I am afraid that _____.

My heart hurts so much because _____.

Today, God, I am asking You to _____ .

Yet, I have hope because I know that You haven't forgotten me and that You are listening to my prayers. While I must wait for Your timing to answer, I will trust in You. Amen.

Today's Takeaway

When I trust that God loves me, I can talk to Him about everything in my heart.

Day 3: Lessons for Living on God's Time Line

Have you ever seen the "The Marshmallow Test" video on YouTube?[10] It's an experiment where preschoolers and early elementary-aged kids are given a single marshmallow and put in a room by themselves. Before leaving the room, an adult tells each child that if he or she can wait, then they will get another marshmallow when time is up. Clip after clip shows the sweet and funny struggles of the kids as they practice waiting. Some of the kids sniff or squeeze the sticky treat. Other kids distract themselves by playing games with their fingers. A few kids can't wait any longer and begin licking or nibbling their marshmallows around the edges. The kids who succeed in waiting stop looking at the marshmallow by putting their heads down on the table or turning their bodies away so they can't see it.

This cute video might feature little kids, but it points to an important reason worship is so important to us waiting well. There are a lot of good "marshmallows" that we really want in life, such as good jobs, a family, fulfilling career, good health, and a chance to live our dreams. The more that we focus on our "marshmallow," the less we focus on God. When you let your heart long for something that you don't or can't have, that longing can actually make your heart sick (Proverbs 13:12). This is why worshiping God while you wait is one of the ways that God can bless you during your waiting room journey.

God's delay in answering our prayers is often the disruption we need. Like the kids who found success by taking their eyes off the marshmallow and focusing on something else, we need to take our eyes off of what won't satisfy us forever and learn how to find satisfaction only in God (Matthew 6:19-21; Psalm 41:1-12).

Today you are going to finish Hannah's story and then apply what you've learned this week to your waiting room journey.

As one who only likes to watch movies with happy endings, I want to believe that Hannah will go home from Shiloh and get pregnant within the next month. After all, she has an incredible encounter with God. Instead, this is what happens next:

> [19]Early the next morning they arose and worshiped before the LORD and then went back to their home at Ramah. Elkanah made love to his wife Hannah, and the LORD

remembered her. [20]*So in the course of time Hannah became pregnant and gave birth to a son. She named him Samuel, saying, "Because I asked the* LORD *for him."*

(1 Samuel 1:19-20)

While Hannah's radical encounter with God transforms her perspective, it does not change her circumstances. I love thinking that Hannah actually enjoys worshiping with God the next morning before they leave Shiloh. I hope that Peninnah's snarky words roll right off Hannah's back as she packs their bags. As their family leaves Shiloh, Hannah has no guarantee that God will give her what she wants. Prayer guides our hearts to God, but our prayers aren't guarantees that God will give us what we want. Even so, she leaves Shiloh deeply blessed because God does save her from hopelessness and despair.

Refer back to 1 Samuel 1:19-20, and circle the phrase "in the course of time."

The phrase "in the course of time" or "in due time" describes an undefined time line, more specifically God's time line. We don't know how long it takes Hannah to get pregnant. Even though Hannah may have still felt sad each passing month, her heart was changed and transformed back at Shiloh. So, even as she remains in her waiting room, she is blessed with more hope and faith than before.

There are times in the Bible when God reveals His time line and other instances when He doesn't. He uses it to accomplish whatever is according to His will. Anytime we experience undefined time lines we are reminded that we don't have control. And we're reminded that it would be wise for us not to try to take control. Since time is a tool for God, He can use it to accomplish the seemingly impossible in our lives.

In Genesis, Abraham and Sarah live with an unanswered prayer for a child, like Elkanah and Hannah. However, Abraham is given the promise that he and his wife will have a son, but he isn't given a time line. Complicating matters is that Abraham is very old and Sarah is beyond the age of childbearing.

Yet, God asks Abraham a question that we must all answer when we're sitting in the waiting room wondering or worrying about our situation.

Read Genesis 18:14 in the margin.

What is the question that God asks Abraham? Fill in the blank:

"Is anything too _____ for the LORD**?"**

"Is anything too hard for the LORD*? I will return to you at the appointed time next year, and Sarah will have a son."*

(Genesis 18:14)

Consider your situation from God's all-powerful position. Is your unanswered prayer too hard for God?

The Hebrew word "difficult" or "hard" is *pala*,[12] which means to be surpassing or extraordinary. Whenever we look at a situation from our view in the waiting room, our perspective is limited. We can only see the solution to our situation through our limited abilities. Yet, God is limitless because He can do the extraordinary.

Even if I know that God can do the impossible, the question that has caused me the most struggle is: Will God do what I am praying that He will do? It's here that my faith in God is tested. Will I wait and trust God's outcome for my life or try to force my own solution?

The difference between Hannah's story and Sarah's story is that Hannah takes her pain and her problem to God, but Sarah cooks up a scheme and takes matters into her own hands. Even though she knows what God has promised, Sarah is tired of waiting. She gives her slave Hagar to Abraham as a second wife because during this time, children born to a servant can be claimed by a barren wife. The result of Sarah trying to be the answer to her problem is disastrous.

Read Genesis 16:3-6, and describe the relationship between the following:

Sarah and Hagar:

Sarah and Abraham:

There are a lot of reasons why we shouldn't try to force solutions. One of the most difficult consequences is the damage to our relationships with others. Hagar harasses Sarah. Then Sarah nags Abraham. Impatience does result in a baby—and a lot of bitter feelings, too.

Even as Sarah and Abraham are impatient, God still honors His promise. Eventually, Sarah gives birth to Abraham's son, Isaac. While Abraham and Sarah finally receive their much-desired son, their inability to wait on God's time line has created hurt and heartache that will flow through many generations to come.

When we push or force our own solutions, God may allow us to have our way. But we have to deal with the consequences, usually in the form of wrecked relationships that leave us asking the question: Was it really worth it? The answer is usually no. So, while God always keeps His promises to us, even when we mess up, it is wise for us to learn from Sarah's example and bypass the temptation to take matters into our own hands.

Sarah, Abraham, and Hagar's story lends itself to an important waiting room warning: When we try to push our way out of a waiting room, we will cause pain and problems in other people's lives.

Can you think of a time when you tried to push your way out of a waiting room and create your own answer to prayer?

How did that situation impact the relationships around you?

What do you think you should you have done instead?

If you've struggled with trying to force solutions or fix others, don't beat yourself up. Now's the time for you to confess your lack of faith or trust to God. Please don't let shame or condemnation define you. Here's more encouragement! Even though Sarah jumps ahead of God, she is still remembered in the New Testament for her faith: "It was by faith that even Sarah was able to have a child, though she was barren and was too old. She believed that God would keep his promise" (Hebrews 11:11 NLT). The takeaway here is that perhaps God is waiting for you to stop trying to fix the situation so that He can work it out.

Eventually, Hannah does get pregnant and gives birth to a son named Samuel. But the point of God answering Hannah's prayer isn't that she receives what she wants; it is that now it's time for God to accomplish a greater purpose through allowing her to get pregnant. Hannah's long waiting room journey is part of God's greater time line. One writer makes

this observation: "Samuel was God's 'bridge builder' at a critical time."[13] Samuel is the last of the judges that God sent to deal with the unfaithful Israelites. Also, Samuel is the prophet who follows Moses (1 Samuel 3:20). Eventually, Samuel appoints the first two kings of Israel, Saul and David.

In my life, it has been helpful to remember that God's outcomes to our situations involve more than just giving us what we want in the here and now. I'm learning that there is an eternal aspect to my deepest unanswered prayer. The better I become at worshiping God in my waiting room, the more of God I reflect in my ministry and relationships with others.

Here are four lessons from Hannah's story. Put a checkmark beside the lesson or lessons that you need to remember today.

_____ 1. An unanswered prayer doesn't mean that God has forgotten you or doesn't love you. (Romans 8:38-39; Jeremiah 31:3)

_____ 2. Bold prayer is a way of letting God know that you trust Him to lead your life. (2 Chronicles 7:14; Ephesians 6:18; 1 John 5:14-15)

_____ 3. Worshiping God strengthens your heart and transforms your attitude while you are waiting. (Isaiah 26:3; Romans 12:1-12)

_____ 4. God's delayed answer to your prayer often involves a larger time line than what is happening in your life. (John 5:17; Romans 8:28)

WAITING ROOM APPLICATION

Waiting to Worshiping

Between the time that Hannah returns from Shiloh and the time that she finally becomes pregnant, how does she live? One day at a time. The path to patience while living with an unanswered prayer isn't found in the future or the past but in today.

Here's a simple tool you can use. Instead of saying, "God, I'm waiting for you to _____," proclaim, "God, I'm worshiping you today for _____." As you worship God by remembering who He is, what

He has already done in your life, or what He promises, you position yourself to be blessed by the presence of God in your life.

Ready to give it a try?

God, I'm not going to focus on waiting; today I choose to worship you for _____

_____.

Prayer

God Almighty, there is nothing too hard for You! Rather than focus on my "marshmallow," God, I turn my heart, my life, and my attention to You. Even as You are powerful enough to do the impossible, I will wait for You in faith and not to try to force solutions. Like Hannah, I give You thanks for who You are and all the blessings You've given me. Instead of waiting and worrying, I will worship you. Amen.

Bible Story Wrap-up

Even though Hannah makes it to the end of that waiting room season in her life, there is more to her story. After her son's birth, she keeps her promise to give him to Eli, the priest, to serve in ministry for the boy's entire life. Hannah goes on to give birth to five more children (1 Samuel 2:20-21). Again, the point of learning about Hannah's life isn't that God gives her a son but that she is a woman of great faith who worships God and prays boldly. Hannah gave back to God before she ever received what she requested, and she continued to live by faith in a way that inspires us today.

Now that we have come to the end of Hannah's story, take a moment to consider what you have learned and how God is calling you to respond.

What are one or two things that you've learned from Hannah's life this week?

How is God prompting you to think or live differently as a result of what you've heard or learned?

Today's Takeaway

Worship lifts the heavy weight of waiting from my heart and mind.

Gratitude Moment

Today I am grateful to God for _____

_____

_____

_____

_____.

Today you have the opportunity to participate in an optional self-study with a Bible verse or passage of your choosing. The Verse Bank on page 143 features Scriptures that fit thematically with Hannah. Select one of the Scriptures listed and follow these prompts.

Read

Write below the verse or passage you selected:

Reflect

Now open your Bible and read a few verses that precede and follow your chosen Scripture in order to gather a bigger picture of what is going on. Use study helps as needed or desired to answer questions such as these: Who is speaking? Who is the audience? When or where were these words written? What is the overarching message? Are there any words that you need to look up for better understanding? (Check out Bible search websites such as BibleGateway.com and others for commentaries, Bible dictionaries, and other tools.) Write your responses below.

Respond

Ask yourself this question: How does God want me to think or live differently as a result of what I've read? Consider how you can apply this passage to your life.

Release

Write a prayer to God expressing that you are willing to apply what you've learned to your life.

Day 5: Devotional and Prayer Journaling
(Optional)

Those who hope in the LORD
*   will renew their strength.*
They will soar on wings like eagles;
*   they will run and not grow weary,*
*   they will walk and not be faint.*
                        (Isaiah 40:31)

Gratitude Moment

Today I am grateful to God for _____

_____

_____

_____

_____.

Unlike her older sister, Tonya dreamed of being a wife and mother from childhood. Even as she pursued her college and graduate education in music and opera performance, Tonya prayed for a husband and a chance to be a mom.

Married in her early thirties, she and her husband devoted their time to raising his young daughter from a first marriage. Being a stepmom increased Tonya's desire to be a mom, even though she knew that they needed more time before they had their own children.

As Tonya approached her fortieth birthday, she tried not to panic. Month after month, nothing happened. While her friends announced pregnancies and births, she worked hard to stay encouraged and upbeat. However, she did admit the heartache to her sister and close friends.

One day Tonya wrote out the words from Isaiah 40:31 and posted them on her computer at work. Those words were a reminder that God would help her endure the long and painful road of infertility.

Just a few verses before Isaiah 40:31, the prophet Isaiah reminds us that God never gets tired or weary, even though we do. In fact, God promises to give power and strength to those who need it (Isaiah 40:29). So, Isaiah 40:31 is a summary of a blessing for those who choose to trust God when waiting rooms and weary roads have no end in sight.

Generally, everything in our world gets worn down when pressure is repeatedly applied. That's why Jesus taught us to build value in what's eternal instead of in material possessions (Matthew 6:19). But it's not just what we see around us that wears out; our hearts and bodies wear down in the face of pain and ongoing problems. Do financial problems, health issues, or relationship issues ever wear you out?

God knows this about us, and that's why Isaiah 40:31 is such a special promise for our lives!

When we trust God in the midst of whatever is pushing on our lives, God uses that pressure to make us stronger, not weaker. Consider the strength imagery Isaiah paints for us: soaring with eagles, running without weariness, and walking without fainting aren't possible in our human strength. Yet God gives us strength beyond our human strength.

This is why, to this day, Tonya leaves that Post-it note with Isaiah 40:31 attached to her computer. It's there to remind her to lean into God's strength when a coworker brings in her children on family days. It's Tonya's reminder when another friend announces a pregnancy on social media. That verse continues to give her strength and courage after test results revealed serious medical issues impacting her fertility.

With the strength that only God can provide, Tonya lives with purpose. She prays boldly for God to give her a child, but she also gives back to God in faith. Tonya participates in her women's Bible study at church and uses her gift of hospitality to serve others in big and small ways. She continues to nurture her musical gift by performing on opera stages in the U.S. and Europe, including Carnegie Hall.

As her older sister, I've witnessed my sister's steadfast faith grow stronger the past few years, even as she has battled crushing heartache. When I asked her permission to share her story and told her the verse I would be using, she sent me a snapshot of Isaiah 40:31 on the front of her computer.

No matter if you are facing a battle with infertility like my sister and Hannah or there is another unanswered prayer in your life, let God renew your heart, mind, and strength today.

Prayer

Dear God, I put my hope and trust in You. Thank You for providing me with the strength that is far beyond what I could have on my own. I am so grateful that You never grow tired and have promised to give me strength when I don't think I can hang in there another day. Amen.

Introducing Prayer Journaling

Journaling, or writing in general, can be intimidating for many. But I am a firm believer that writing out our prayers not only helps us focus our distracted minds on God but also provides us with tangible, written milestones that testify to God's work in our lives. Right now there are stacks of journals in my home that testify to how God has changed and transformed my heart. Those prayers encourage me as I make my way through circumstances of unanswered prayer.

My prayer is that if you pull out this study six months or a year from now and look at what you've written, you'll celebrate how God used it to strengthen your faith, create new courage, and help you experience the kind of joy and peace that you've deeply desired.

Each week I'll include some prompts with the Day 5 Devotional that you can use to get started. Just give it a try!

Prayer Journaling Prompts

As you reflect on this week's study of Hannah and the lessons that you've learned, what do you need to talk with God about today? Where have you been patient in waiting? What makes you impatient? Where do you struggle with prayer?

Consider the lessons that you've learned from Hannah. How do you resonate with her story? What have you sensed God speaking to you?

As you write out your prayer today, talk with God about any specific action steps He is calling you to take in order to claim greater faith in your waiting room situation.

Hannah

From Waiting to Worshiping

We're blessed when we turn our waiting into worship.

Welcome/Prayer/Icebreaker (5-10 minutes)

Welcome to Session 1 of I'm Waiting, God. Over the next four weeks we're going to take a look at four women in the Bible who endured a long season of sadness, pain, and waiting and who show us how we can develop the faith to wait on God when our prayers are not being answered according to our time line or agenda. This week we've considered what it's like when our prayers are unanswered and we feel like God has forgotten us. Today we're exploring what Hannah has to teach us about turning our waiting into worship so that we might experience God's blessing. Take a moment to open with prayer, and then go around the circle and share what you generally do to help pass the time when you're waiting.

Video (about 20 minutes)

Play the Group Centering video for Week 1 (optional), taking a couple of minutes to focus your hearts and minds on God and God's Word. Then play the video segment for Week 1, filling in the blanks as you watch and making notes about anything that resonates with you or that you want to be sure to remember.

—Video Notes—

Scriptures: Psalm 84:11, Psalm 37:4, Matthew 7:7, 1 Samuel 1:7-8,
1 Samuel 1:10, James 5:16, 1 Samuel 1:11, Hebrews 4:16,
1 Samuel 1:18, 1 Samuel 1:20

You are blessed when you discover that you have the freedom to be
_____ with how you _____ before God.

You are blessed when you boldly ask God for what you really _____
and fully _____ Him to give you want you need.

You are blessed each time you proclaim, "I'm _____ You,
God, for…" instead of saying, "I'm waiting on You, God, to…"

Other Insights:

Group Discussion (20-25 minutes for a 60-minute session; 30-35 minutes for a 90-minute session)

Video Discussion

- When you are in the midst of difficult circumstances, do you ever find it difficult to believe that God is with you and for you—that God loves you, even when you're angry with Him and He isn't punishing you? Explain your response.
- How easy is it for you to be real with God about how you feel? How easy is it for you to be real with others about how you feel?
- What does it look like to pray boldly and then give back before we receive?
- How can the two-sided prayer help us to test our motives when we pray?
- How might you move from waiting on God to worshiping God?

Workbook Discussion

- How does Hannah's story resonate with you?
- What have you been praying for that hasn't happened yet, and what emotions are you feeling as you wait? (page 40)
- *"Holding on to a healthy perspective when experiencing God's delay is crucial to not missing a blessing that God wants you to experience"* (page 18). What three things does a healthy perspective remember? (pages 18–19) How would remembering these things help you keep a healthy perspective when you're waiting on God?
- Read 1 Samuel 1:9-10. How is Hannah described as praying? (page 21) What do you imagine that scene to be like? What was Hannah feeling? What did it look like? What did it sound like?
- When was the last time you told God what was really on your heart and mind when you were upset with Him? How would you describe that experience?
- *"Your view of God determines how you might approach or shy away from Him in prayer"* (page 24). How did you view God and prayer as a child? How have those views expanded?

- Read 1 Samuel 1:20. When have you experienced an "in the course of time" season as you waited on God? Reflect on that season and share a moment when you saw God working, even in the waiting.
- What did you discover this week about the similarities between Sarah's (Genesis 16:3-6) and Hannah's experiences of waiting on God for answers to their prayers?
- Can you think of a time when you tried to push your way out of a waiting room and create your own answer to prayer? (page 29) How has that worked for you?
- Hannah received her answer to prayer and gave birth to her son Samuel. What did Hannah promise God she would do with her son? What did you learn about Samuel's leadership in the greater story of God?
- Look at the four lessons from Hannah's story on page 30. Which of the lessons speak to your current season in prayer right now? Why?
- *"When we trust God in the midst of whatever is pushing on our lives, God uses that pressure to make us stronger, not weaker"* (page 34). How do you respond to this statement? Looking back on your life with God, when can you see that pressure made you stronger to face your challenges?

Learning to Wait (10-15 minutes – 90-minute session only)

Divide into groups of two or three and discuss the following (see page 31):

- What are one or two things you've learned from Hannah's life this week?
- How is God prompting you to think or live differently as a result of what you've heard or learned?

Closing Prayer (5 minutes)

Close the session by sharing personal prayer requests and praying together. If you like, invite the women to surround those who have shared requests and pray for them aloud. In addition to praying aloud for one another, close by asking God to help you pray boldly, worship bravely, and believe confidently that He is with you and for you even in the midst of a season of waiting.

Week 2

Ruth

God, Now What?

(Ruth 1–4)

Memory Verse

Be joyful in hope, patient in affliction, faithful in prayer.
(Romans 12:12)

There are many different ways that we can characterize seasons of unanswered prayers. Last week we explored Hannah's story using the analogy of a waiting room. Although the waiting room will continue to be an overarching image throughout our study, this week we're adding "unexpected journey" as a metaphor since the woman whose life we're following experienced many difficult and unexpected off-road moments in her life.

I travel a lot as a Bible teacher and author, and I've learned to embrace the unexpected—like the time when I landed in the U.S. from an overseas speaking engagement and there was a skirmish in the security section. Quick action by the airport staff prevented an all-out riot. After the chaos settled, my travel companion and I had to take off our flip slips and race through the airport against the clock to make our connecting flight home. We arrived two minutes too late. After twelve hours of travel, we slumped against the departure gate counter dirty, tired, and stranded far from home. I remember feeling a flash of anger and a flood of it's-not-fair feelings. My unexpected journey tested my patience and attitude. It was hard practicing patience when tired, hot, and dirty!

If you've ever experienced a canceled flight, road detour, or any other travel delay, those moments can upset the most carefully laid plans. Even though our current technology can warn us of upcoming slowdowns and offer alternative routes, we still can't prevent those moments from happening. What matters is how we manage ourselves through those moments.

What's the unexpected, off-road situation you're asking God to fix today? Is it an unexpected job loss? Has a child or loved one made some bad decisions that have thrown their lives into chaos? Has a parent or friend received an unexpected diagnosis that will permanently alter their quality of life?

As much as God tells us to walk by faith through the unknown and unexpected, it's not an easy journey. One of the lessons that I've learned over the years is to hold on to God, look for others who have walked the road ahead of me, and learn from them. One of those women that I've learned a lot from is a woman named Ruth in the Old Testament.

Gratitude Moment

Today I am grateful to God for _____

_____

_____

_____.

WAITING ROOM PROBLEM

What do you do when unexpected events throw your life off course?

Ruth's story comes before Hannah's story in the Bible. It's found right after the Book of Judges, which ends after reporting one of the most heinous, deplorable events in the Bible involving the brutal abuse and death of a woman at the hands of the Benjamites, one of the tribes of Israel (Judges 19–21). This tragedy shows just how far the Israelites' hearts had moved away from God during the time of the judges of Israel. Then right after Ruth's story is 1 Samuel that begins with Hannah's story, which we explored last week. While Hannah endured a lengthy waiting room journey, her long-awaited Samuel would be the "bridge-builder" God gave the Israelites to invite their hearts back to Him.

With this general biblical time line for context, let's jump into Ruth's story, which actually is the story of two women, Ruth and Naomi. Today we're going to look at the different attitudes of these two women facing the same difficult circumstance. If you know that you are struggling with a less-than-positive attitude toward God or your situation, I am so glad that you are here. God doesn't want to criticize or condemn you; so take in today's lesson and let it encourage and perhaps challenge your heart to change because of God's faithfulness.

Naomi will show us what it looks like to struggle with pain and bitterness. And Ruth will show us how to respond in faith when life takes an unexpected or unwanted detour. If you've ever felt like your life is stuck in a traffic jam, broken down by the side of the road, or stranded in an airport far from home, God has a blessing in store for you this week. As you dive into Ruth's story, you'll see that God can redeem any person, rebuild every hope, and restore a beautiful legacy for the future.

Read Ruth 1:1-5, and fill in the blanks.

1. Due to a famine, a Jewish man named _____

   moves his wife, _____, and two sons,

   _____ and _____,

   from Bethlehem to Moab.

2. Elimelek _____, and Naomi's sons marry

   Moabite women named _____ and

   _____.

3. After about ten years, Mahlon and Kilion also

   _____, leaving Naomi without her husband

   and her two sons.

The Book of Ruth opens with a Jewish man, Elimelek, leaving Beth-lehem in Judah because of a famine, quite possibly because of the people's disobedience. (According to Leviticus 26:14-20, God allowed hardships such as famine to spread across the Promised Land both as a consequence for sin as well as an opportunity for His people to repent and turn back to Him). Unlike Abraham, who was specifically called to move away by God (Genesis 12:1-3), Elimelek leaves the Promised Land that God had given His people many years before and moves his family east to Moab, an idol-worshiping country whose name means "waste" or "nothingness."[1]

While there is much to cover in Ruth's story, let's take a moment to ponder Elimelek's actions. Does the grumbling in his stomach or fear of his family's starvation cause him to question God's faithfulness? Does Elimelek give God a deadline and then take matters into his own hands? I ask these questions because I can imagine his tension: "God, we've been hungry a long time and I don't want my family to starve. If you don't do something, then I'm going to deal with this myself."

We don't know the answers to these questions, but we do know that Elimelek leaves the place of God's blessing and settles in a place that is far from God. One of the consequences of Elimelek's actions is that his sons marry Moabite women, a practice God warned the Israelites against (Deuteronomy 7:3-4) because the women would woo their hearts from serving God. In fact, Moabite women had a notorious history for doing such a thing (Numbers 25).[2]

Then, Elimelek dies there in godless Moab, followed by the deaths of his sons. A tragic end to a man born into a covenant in which God himself promises to take care of His people when they trust Him. In the end, Naomi is widowed and suffering in a personal famine of her own. She is now without the provision that a husband provides. She is also childless, with no legacy or protection for the future.

I can almost hear Naomi and Ruth cry, "God, now what?"

Read Ruth 1:6. What does Naomi hear?

Once she learns that God has provided food once again to His people, Naomi and her widowed daughters-in-law, Ruth and Orpah (not Oprah!), get on the road to return to Naomi's homeland in Judah. But as they get on the road, Naomi changes her mind.

Read Ruth 1:8-16, and answer the questions below:

In verses 8, 11, and 12, what does Naomi tell Ruth and Orpah to do?

Look at verse 8. What word does Naomi use to describe how Ruth and Orpah have treated her?

Naomi's words to her daughters-in-law are so sweet to me. As a stereotype, mother-in-law and daughter-in-law relationships are often portrayed as passive-aggressive or even outright aggressive. However, Naomi lavishes gratitude on Ruth and Naomi, with whom she has shared a lot of life experience. Knowing what they've all been through, the women likely provide many days of comfort to one another.

I wonder if Ruth and Orpah comfort Naomi as she prays to return to Bethlehem—and if Naomi comforts her daughters-in-law as they remain childless?

When our prayers go unanswered, one of God's most beautiful blessings is someone who comforts us. Likewise, another blessing is that we are able to comfort others. The longer I live with unanswered prayer, the more aware I've become of the people God wants me to pray for and the opportunities I have to show them love and hope in Jesus' name.

Read 2 Corinthians 1:4-5 in the margin. How does God's comfort motivate us to reach out and help others when they struggle?

⁴He comforts us in all our troubles so that we can comfort others. When they are troubled, we will be able to give them the same comfort God has given us.⁵For the more we suffer for Christ, the more God will shower us with his comfort through Christ.

(2 Corinthians 1:4-5 NLT)

In Ruth 1:11-14, Naomi lays out the argument for why her daughters-in-law should abandon her and return to Moab. How would you describe Naomi's attitude toward her situation?

What does Orpah do?

What does Ruth decide to do?

Can you imagine this emotional scene between the three women who've been through so much loss and unfulfilled dreams together? Naomi is leaving empty-handed from a godless land that has swallowed the bodies of her husband and sons. She also has watched as the childless Ruth and Orpah have buried and grieved their husbands.

If I could, I'd like to have a friend-to-friend moment with you to share two important things:

1. *You have permission to grieve when your life changes, whether for better or worse.* Denying or minimizing what you've been through will actually rob you of God's full and complete healing. It's okay to ignore others' comments such as, "You shouldn't feel bad about that," or "Oh, you'll get over that." Go ahead and feel those feelings.
2. *Your feelings are real, but they're not reliable.* As you feel those honest, hurtful, uncomfortable, or unnamed emotions, you don't have to let them be in charge of your attitudes or actions. Let God's truth re-direct your feelings so that you can make healthy and wise decisions for your future.

Unfortunately, Naomi has a lot of really strong feelings driving her conversation with her daughters-in-law. Naomi tells the women that they have a better chance at a future if they return home to their false gods than if they follow Naomi back to Judah, a place where people have a chance to worship the almighty, all-powerful God.

It's here that Ruth makes her famous and passionate response to Naomi's pleas to return back to Moab.

> ¹⁶Ruth replied, "Don't ask me to leave you and turn back. Wherever you go, I will go; wherever you live, I will live. Your people will be my people, and your God will be my God. ¹⁷Wherever you die, I will die, and there I will be buried. May the LORD punish me severely if I allow anything but death to separate us!"
>
> (Ruth 1:16-17 NLT)

What do you learn from Ruth's spiritual declaration in these verses?

Ruth chooses to move forward in faith with Naomi, using words that point to expectation and wonder. She's not harboring blame or even resentment toward Naomi or God. Even as Moab is a godless country and even though Elimelek left the place of God's promise to make his own way in Moab, God worked it all together to draw Ruth to Him. Likewise, even when we fail to be faithful, God is at work accomplishing His purpose and drawing other willing hearts toward Himself.

Ruth, a Moabite woman, chooses a new path, people, and sovereign power. Even after her husband has died, she doesn't abandon her faith or Naomi just because their lives have detoured into a ditch. Instead, she shows faithfulness to Naomi and God. One commentator says it like this: "In spite of the bad example of her disobedient in-laws, Ruth had come to know the true and living God, and she wanted to be with His people and dwell in His land."⁴

So the two women set off to travel the long way back without husbands, children, or grandchildren. They may not have had many possessions, but I suspect that they lugged along pretty heavy hearts. Once the two women travel the thirty to fifty miles from Moab to Bethlehem, their return is noticed and causes quite a scene.

Read Ruth 1:19-20. What does Naomi tell the Bethlehem women to call her?

Who does she blame for her bitter attitude?

Naomi's name means pleasant,[5] but she announces to the women in Bethlehem that she wants to be called Mara, which means bitter. Notice how she says "because the Almighty has made my life very bitter" (v. 20). In this verse, the Hebrew for "Almighty" is *El Shaddai*. Naomi's bitterness seems to come from the expectation that a powerful God could have stopped the pain and loss in her life. Since He didn't, Naomi is bitter.

Bitterness is when we submerge ourselves in anger and self-pity. Bitterness might sound a lot like Naomi's, "God let this happen to me." To be clear, our bitterness can't stop God's sovereignty, but it does suffocate the flow of God's power in our lives.

When we face the unexpected or there appears to be a delay in the answer to our prayers, we must be on-guard against bitterness. Our minds naturally drift toward the negative; and without intentionally saturating our minds with God's promises, we'll drift into daily retelling ourselves the story of what we've lost, what went wrong, how we've been hurt, and where God has failed us. In time, those stories drip the poison of bitterness into our hearts. It's an acid that burns holes in our holiness and weakens our faith.

One of the most well-known verses on bitterness is found in Hebrews 12:15. The writer uses Esau's story as an example of the danger of bitterness. Esau was Abraham's grandson, son of the long-awaited Isaac whom you read about briefly last week. As the oldest of twins, Esau was entitled to the family inheritance and spiritual leadership of the family. His younger twin, Jacob, exploited a weakness in Esau's character in order to swindle his brother out of those blessings. Years later, God wrestled with Jacob over his deceptive nature, and his heart was changed. However, the New Testament records a different outcome for Esau's legacy.

> [15]*Look after each other so that none of you fails to receive the grace of God. Watch out that no poisonous root of bitterness grows up to trouble you, corrupting many.* [16]*Make sure that no one is immoral or godless like Esau, who traded his birthright as the firstborn son for a single meal.* [17]*You know that afterward, when he wanted his father's blessing, he was rejected. It was too late for repentance, even though he begged with bitter tears.*

> (*Hebrews* 12:15-17 NLT)

On the previous page, circle the phrase "root of bitterness."

Why was Esau bitter?

These verses point to the root of bitterness, which grows when we reject God's path and then blame Him for the losses and pain in our lives.

Before I was born, my grandfather had a long-term extramarital affair leading to my grandparents' divorce. The trauma of the affair and the fallout pushed my Christian grandmother deep into a sea of bitterness. Her pain and anger were so great that her physical health failed. During much of my childhood, she stayed in the hospital suffering from bleeding ulcers. The fallout also meant that we had little to no relationship with our grandfather for many years. Gratefully, my grandmother decided to renew her relationship with God, which led her to forgive my grandfather. That decision to release her bitterness actually changed the trajectory of our family history in a positive way.

By the end of our time with Ruth's story, we will see Naomi travel that road back to God as well, but for now we will end today with a quick temperature check for you.

Temperature Check

A = always, S = Sometimes, N = Never

Circle A, S, or N for each statement:

1. I am upset or bitter with God over my current situation.
   A   S   N

2. I feel it's not fair that I am paying the price for someone else's mistake.
   A   S   N

3. I am afraid that I will stay stuck in this waiting room forever.
   A   S   N

4. It feels like the best days of my life are behind me.
   A   S   N

5. I want to turn away from my bitterness.

    A   S   N

6. I feel like giving up on what I'm waiting for.

    A   S   N

Prayer

God, I want to be like Ruth and follow You in faith even when my life detours in a ditch. You are a God who promises to never leave us or forsakes us (Joshua 1:4-5), and You will provide what we need when we trust in You (Matthew 6:33). God, help me hold on to these promises so that I will follow in faith and righteousness, not fear and bitterness. As I am praying, I feel I may need to release bitterness toward _____

_____ (person) or _____

(circumstance) because I've not received what I've been praying for.

Today, I choose to intentionally remember Your promises to me.
You promise to never leave me or forsake me (Hebrews 13:5).
You promise to provide for my needs (Philippians 4:19).
You promise to give me strength and courage to endure (Joshua 1:9).

I will hold on to these promises and repeat them whenever anger or bitterness tempts me to turn away from You; in Jesus' name. Amen.

Day 2: Living by Faith in the Messy Middle

WAITING ROOM PRINCIPLE

The way you live with an unanswered prayer is a powerful part of your testimony.

While working in the corporate world, I dreamed of helping teenagers and young mothers finish their education. As a wife and nineteen-year-old mom, I knew how hard it was to get a degree and raise kids while growing up myself. Eventually, an opportunity opened up for me to leave my pharmaceutical sales career and become the executive director of a nonprofit helping young, single moms. The nonprofit was located in my neighborhood. I would no longer need to travel and, best of all, I could bring my third and youngest daughter to work with me each day. So, after months of praying and seeking counsel with family and friends, I felt like God gave the green light for this opportunity.

However, things got rocky really fast. On my first day, the building's furnace broke down. As the months went on, I had to replace staff and deal with a burglary and client struggles. I took that job to make a difference, but every day I woke up feeling defeated. I second-guessed my decision to leave my successful career every day. I felt like I was failing my family every day. I struggled with tremendous shame because I felt like I failed God, too. Did I hear you wrong, God? I thought this was the direction you wanted me to go.

After one year I left the position feeling very defeated. Once I'd been an award-winning sales representative. Now I felt like a failure. For the next year, I floundered. Tears flowed all day, every day.

In His mercy, God led me to a small group of women at my church who had embarked upon a year-long leadership and discipleship program. As our community began learning and growing together, their iron re-sharpened my tear-rusted iron. I started floundering less as my faith flourished more. Praise God that I stopped flopping around in self-pity and developed a laser focus for studying God's Word.

Along the unexpected and unwanted journey was where I learned that I had to let go of my expectations and lean into trusting the new direction where God was leading me. As I moved toward God, He led me into new attitudes, beliefs, and behaviors that ultimately blessed me with new freedom and an amazing new purpose. Today I look back on that season of life and shout amen to the psalmist who declared, "God's way is perfect. / All the Lord's promises prove true. / He is a shield for all who look to him for protection" (Psalm 18:30 NLT).

Today we're going to look at how Ruth navigates the next step in her unexpected journey. She has arrived in a new town as a young, widowed woman from another country. What's a girl to do in that situation? Ruth's attitude and behavior point to three lessons of faithfulness and obedience that we'll explore today.

Read Ruth 2:1-3.

What does Ruth ask Naomi's permission to do?

Who owns the field that Ruth ends up working in?

Extra Insights

Barley season begins in April/May.[6]

Ruth's request to Naomi demonstrates that she is one gutsy gal! She asks to go to work and find food for their survival, even though she knows that as a woman and a foreigner she might be unwelcome or harassed. Imagine if you moved to a small rural town in a different country. Not only would you look different than everyone else, but you also would not know the language. On top of all of those barriers, you would have nothing and need to rely upon the goodwill of strangers to survive.

As we know from Ruth's well-known speech to Naomi, she has made a declaration of faith and her willingness to follow God. So, it seems in this space between living in an unknown land and going to work in uncertain conditions, Ruth chooses to focus on trusting God and believing He will provide.

As Ruth begins working in the field, we find out that she happens to show up in the fields of a man named Boaz, whose name means "in him is strength."[7] Of course, Ruth thinks that she is working in some random field. However, God's greater plan unfolds as she is picking up leftovers and wondering what will happen next in her life.

God commanded His people to provide for the poor and widowed by allowing them to glean or pick up food that had fallen from the baskets of the field workers as well as the unpicked growth around the edges (see Leviticus 19:9-10).

Read Ruth 2:4-12. In verse 4, what does Boaz's greeting to his workers tell you about his character and faith?

This greeting is noteworthy because in Ruth and Boaz's time, there were no leaders, judges, or prophets to lead God's people. As mentioned previously, the Book of Judges records the heartbreaking decisions and actions of people whose hearts had moved far from God. Yet here is evidence that not all had turned away from trusting God. Boaz was a man who still trusted God and followed the covenant commands.

Boaz is also a man who knows what is happening in his fields. He notices Ruth.

What are four things the overseer shares about his conversation with Ruth?

1.

2.

3.

4.

First, the overseer tells Boaz that Ruth is a Moabite, which could trigger some negative feelings considering the history between the two countries. Second, he mentions that Ruth is with Naomi, which indicates a familiar connection. Third, the overseer shares his conversation with Ruth, including her request to work. And fourth, the overseer gives his observation of Ruth's work ethic. She works hard. She's not out there making excuses or being lazy. Ruth works hard even though she has no idea how the future days of her life will unfold.

As we reflect on the overseer's report on Ruth, another important lesson arises: The way that you live with unanswered prayer is a powerful part of your testimony. A testimony isn't about living so that others are impressed; rather, a testimony is unspoken but action-based evidence of where and what you put your faith in.

If you're in the midst of an unplanned or unexpected detour in life and God hasn't answered your prayers, what kind of testimony might your life be speaking to the people around you?

What are the words that you'd like to be attached to your testimony?

After Boaz talks to his overseer, he talks to Ruth.

Read Ruth 2:8-9, and mark the following statements true (T) or false (F).

_____ Boaz addresses Ruth by saying, "My sister."

_____ He instructs Ruth to leave and work in someone else's field.

_____ Ruth is to work with the other women.

_____ When Ruth is thirsty, she's supposed to drink from the dirty river.

Only the third statement is true. Not only is Boaz the one God sends to faithful Ruth to provide a safe place for her to gather food for survival, but he also is a symbolic figure of God's protection and provision for us all. God will send people to help us, but we will miss the blessing of those people if we're bitter, angry, or looking for rescue in all the wrong places.

Read Ruth 2:10-13. What kind of godly testimony does Ruth establish while still living in godless Moab?

Boaz hears about Ruth's loyalty and faithfulness to Naomi. He knows that Ruth suffered the loss of her husband and was brave enough to move from Moab to Bethlehem where she would be scrutinized by others. How does Ruth respond to Boaz's assessment of her testimony? She falls to the ground and expresses wonder and gratefulness that she has found favor in a place where she doesn't expect it.

Read Ruth 2:14-23, and fill in the blanks below.

Boaz invites Ruth to _____ bread and gives her roasted grain.

When she goes back out to work, Boaz tells the men to let Ruth _____ from the sheaves and not to hassle her.

Ruth collects an _____ of barley, which equals about 26 quarts.[8]

As we read about Boaz, it's easy to see why he's often held up as a virtuous man. Boaz gives Ruth a filling meal after a long day in the field. Then he makes her promises, offers her protection, and provides for her survival. Boaz is a living, breathing symbol of God's grace. I love how one author writes: "The channel of that grace was Boaz. How good it is to know that God has good people living in bad times!"[9] In Ruth's life, Boaz is a flesh-and-bones symbolic reminder of how God looks after us in tough times, even when we don't deserve it.

When we end up on an unplanned life journey, God often sends unexpected, new people into our lives. Are there people in your life who are like Boaz to you?

When Ruth returns home to Naomi that evening, she brings not only a lot of food but also the wonderful owner of the field who treated her, a foreigner, with compassion and kindness. Can you see the light in Ruth's eyes as she reassures Naomi that they won't starve in the days to come?

What does Naomi tell Ruth about Boaz in Ruth 2:20?

What phrase does Naomi use to describe Boaz's obligation to their family?

Not only is Boaz a close relative; he is also their *goel*, a Hebrew word translated as a guardian-redeemer or kinsman-redeemer.[10] In Leviticus 25, God gave instructions for what should happen if a fellow Israelite becomes poor and unable to support themselves, which describes Naomi's situation. As a family member, Boaz was a close relative that would be called upon to step up and assist. Based on what Ruth told her about Boaz, Naomi knows that he will honor his God-given duty (Ruth 2:20).

It is in this dialogue that we see a subtle shift in Naomi's attitude toward God. Before she was bitter, and now she recognizes the kindness of God to her family.

We don't know how Boaz and Naomi's late husband are related. We just know that they are. This becomes important, because after Ruth works in the fields for the remaining weeks of the barley and wheat harvests, Naomi hatches a bold plan. We'll pick up with that in tomorrow's study.

To wrap up today, stop and consider the testimony that you are living right now whether you feel like you are hanging out in a waiting room or traveling an unexpected journey in life.

My Testimony of Living with Unanswered Prayer

Complete the following prompts:

1. For _____ (how long) I've been praying to

   God about _____.

2. While I've been waiting for God to answer my prayer, I feel

   that He _____.

3. The hardest or most painful times of waiting happen when

   _____.

4. Some of my favorite Bible verses that give me hope and help
   me keep my eyes on God are:

5. I am grateful that God has sent _____

   (name/s) into my life to help me. They have blessed me

   because they _____.

6. While I am waiting for God to answer my prayer, I am grateful

   that He has _____.

7. When I think about how others will see my testimony, I hope

   that they will look at my season of unanswered prayer and

   say that I was _____.

Prayer

Dear God, I want to live faithfully like Ruth. Even though she didn't know what her future would look like, she kept living by faith. As I think about the words that I want to be a part of my testimony—such as _____, _____, and _____—give me the faith to live out those words, even on the hard days; in Jesus' name. Amen.

Today's Takeaway

How I live by faith today is an important part of my life's storyline for the rest of my tomorrows.

Day 3: Steps of Obedience and Faith

The next part of Ruth and Naomi's story reads like a mash-up of reality television meets the Hallmark Channel. Let's get right into it.

Read Ruth 3:1-6. What is the purpose of Naomi's plan?

Where does she tell Ruth to look for Boaz that evening?

How is Ruth to prepare?

Ruth is to remain hidden until Boaz has finished doing what?

What curious thing is Ruth supposed to do next?

Write out Ruth's answer to Naomi's instructions below:

Extra Insight

In the Jewish tradition, the Old Testament Book of Ruth is read at the end of the seven-week harvest season during a joyful occasion known as *Shavuot,* or Festival of Weeks (Deuteronomy 16:10-12). It's also been referred to as the Harvest Festival (Exodus 23:16).[11]

So, how would you respond if those were Naomi's instructions to you? Even by today's standards, it feels really forward. For a woman who was in a bitter mood, Naomi knows how to get things moving in the right direction! Or, could it be that in the weeks and months of seeing Ruth bring home food each day and reconnecting with family and friends, perhaps Naomi has let go of some of her bitterness. Now, instead of bitterness over the past, she's taking charge to make sure that Ruth has a secure future.

But why would Naomi give Ruth such bold instructions? I've paraphrased theologian Warren Wiersbe's observations about this below.

He observes that Naomi's plan equips Ruth to symbolically prepare for marriage to a man who hasn't proposed:

1. **Wash** – During that time water was scarce. However, Naomi's instruction to Ruth parallels Moses' instructions to the Israelites to wash themselves and their clothes before sacred events (Genesis 35:1-3), as well as parallels a bride preparing for her wedding.

2. **Put on perfume** – As expected, perfumes would make Ruth smell good and, as Wiersbe says, "nice to be near." This would be a good thing because Ruth would come to Boaz in the night, and her pleasing scent would distinguish her in the dark from the other people on the threshing floor.

3. **Dress in your best clothes** – Ruth likely dressed as a widow and wore those clothes in the dirty fields, but Naomi told her to put off her old clothes. It was now time for Ruth to put on her best clothes as a symbol of a new season in her life.[12]

Why do you think that Ruth follows through on Naomi's instructions?

Ruth's obedience is amazing! She doesn't argue with Naomi or second-guess her plan. Ruth's response is really the fruit of her faithfulness, which even Boaz noticed when he saw her working in the fields. Ruth trusts God and listens to the trusted voices in her life, such as Naomi and Boaz.

Now it's time to find out what happens next!

Read Ruth 3:7-9 and answer the questions:

What kind of mood is Boaz in after eating and drinking?

How does he behave toward Ruth when he wakes up in the night and realizes that she is at his feet?

Why does Ruth ask Boaz to spread his robe over her?

Imagine Boaz waking up in the middle of the night and, instead of smelling unwashed bodies of men who had been working hard at threshing wheat, he smells a lovely scent. Ruth's faithfulness and obedience prepare her to answer Boaz's question with an act of trust and submission when she asks him to spread his robe over her.

The word *robe* (CEB), or garment in some translations, comes from the Hebrew word meaning wing. According to levirate, or religious law, spreading his robe would mean that Boaz would acknowledge Ruth as his wife.[13]

Why hadn't Boaz proposed to Ruth already? In Ruth 3:10-12, Boaz gives two reasons why. What are those reasons?

1.

2.

Boaz's explanation reminds me that even when we're waiting, God is working in the lives of others! Interestingly enough, Boaz is interested but assumes that he isn't what Ruth wants. However, when Naomi presents a faith-based plan, Ruth acts in obedience and faith. Then she discovers that God has been working things out all along the way.

There are times in our waiting rooms or unexpected journeys when we will have to step out and take bold steps of courageous faith. But, how can you know when you're called to make a bold move or when you're trying to push or control the situation?

Here is an exercise that you can do as a way to determine if God might be preparing you to make a bold move even though you're still waiting on an answer to prayer in some area of your life. Even if you aren't considering a bold move, this is a good self-reflection exercise to make sure that you're in position in case a bold move is necessary in the future.

Am I Prepared to Make a Bold Move?

1. Am I letting God lead me each day?

Yes   No   Sometimes

If you are spending time in prayer, silent reflection, and Scripture, you're creating space for the Holy Spirit to flow in and through you. It is God's Holy Spirit that leads you to God's truth in your situation and as provides divine guidance. Even when you don't get turn-by-turn instructions, you can make your way through the messy middle in confident faith that you're trusting God to lead you.

What stops me from feeling fully connected to God?

2. Do I have trusted voices that echo God's Word in my life?

Yes   No   Sometimes

When you have Jesus-loving people in your life who really know you—your desires and dreams as well as your struggles—then they are a great sounding board when you're thinking of making big moves while you are waiting for God to answer your prayer.

Who are the trusted voices in my life? Am I tapping into their wisdom enough? Am I being completely honest with them about my struggle?

3. Do I consistently say "yes" to what God asks me to do?

Yes   No   Sometimes

Part of your waiting journey is learning to be faithful to God in the everyday things—summed up as loving Him with all of your heart, mind, soul, and body as well as loving others (Luke 16:10; Mark 12:30). Though steadfast faithfulness isn't a way to get God to give you what you want, faithfulness will bless you—because our obedience not only blesses us but also powers us up for whatever God has next for us (Luke 11:28; James 1:25).

Where do you struggle to be consistently obedient?

4. If you're letting God lead, listening to trusted voices, and walking in faithful obedience, then is there a step of faith that you sense God calling you to make?

Read Proverbs 16:9 below:

> In their hearts humans plan their course,
> but the LORD establishes their steps.

WAITING ROOM APPLICATION

Here are some steps that God might be inviting you to take in this waiting season of your life:

If you're out of your comfort zone, God invites you to take a *step of faith*.

If you aren't getting what you want, God invites you to take a *step of surrender*.

If your plan is delayed, God invites you to take a *step of patience*.

If you've made a mistake, God invites you to take a *step of humility*.

If a friend or family member fails you, God invites you to take a *step of forgiveness*.

If you've fallen into sin, God invites you to take a *step of repentance*.

Which of these steps might be a bold next step for your life right now?

Prayer

Dear God, I am praying over the steps of faith that You might be calling me to make today. Of all of the steps, I need to take action by _____.

God, as much as I want to be in charge of how my life goes, Ruth's story teaches me that You are in charge of my steps. This is a good thing for me because when You are in charge, then I know that You will lead me down a road toward blessing, even if it's rocky and painful along the way; in Jesus' name. Amen.

Today's Takeaway

An unplanned journey can't stop God from pouring unexpected blessings into your life.

Bible Story Wrap-Up

If you'd like to read the rest of Ruth's story, it won't take long! Check out the final chapter. Ruth 4 contains a sweet story of how Boaz fulfills his spiritual duty and marries Ruth (Ruth 4:13). When their first child is born, the women in the community celebrate with Naomi. Boaz and Ruth's son, Obed, would grow up to become the grandfather of King David.

What fascinates me is that Ruth was a foreign woman whose life detoured in a ditch, yet as she was actively obedient in following God, He took her down a new path, giving her a new life and making her a part of our eternal family. What a tremendous blessing!

Now that we have come to the end of Ruth's story, take a moment to consider what you have learned and how God is calling you to respond.

What are one or two things that you've learned from Ruth's life this week?

How is God prompting you to think or live differently as a result of what you've heard or learned this week?

Day 4: Self-Study (Optional)

Today you have the opportunity to participate in an optional self-study with a Bible verse or passage of your choosing. The Verse Bank on

page 144 features Scriptures hat fit thematically with Ruth. Select one of the Scriptures listed and follow these prompts..

Gratitude Moment

Today I am grateful to God for _____

_____

_____

_____

_____.

Read

Write below the verse or passage you selected:

Reflect

Now open your Bible and read a few verses that precede and follow your chosen Scripture in order to gather a bigger picture of what is going on. Use study helps as needed or desired to answer questions such as these: Who is speaking? Who is the audience? When or where were these words written? What is the overarching message? Are there any words that you need to look up for better understanding? (Check out Bible search websites such as BibleGateway.com and others for commentaries, Bible dictionaries, and other tools.) Write your responses below.

Respond

Ask yourself the question: How does God want me to think or live differently as a result of what I've read? Consider how you can apply this passage to your life.

Release

Write a prayer to God expressing that you are willing to apply what you've learned to your life.

Day 5: Devotional and Prayer Journaling
(Optional)

³He will not let your foot slip—
　　he who watches over you will not slumber;
⁴indeed, he who watches over Israel
　　will neither slumber nor sleep.
⁵The LORD watches over you—
　　the LORD is your shade at your right hand.
　　　　　　(Psalm 121:3-5)

Gratitude Moment

Today I am grateful to God for _____

_____

_____

_____

_____.

A few years ago, I competed in an obstacle course 5K race with my friend Karen. We started out on an easy pace, enjoying the scenic path in the woods. After a mile, we entered a clearing and encountered our first challenge, which was jumping into a deep, muddy pond. I didn't realize that I'd be swimming fully clothed across a muddy pond. And since I only swim once or twice a year, I talked with God a lot about not letting me drown while I swam across the water. It seemed that the edge of the pond extended much farther than the energy I had to swim to it.

By the time I reached the edge of the pond, a lot of my tears mixed with the dirty water splashing over my face. As my hands reached up to grab the top of the muddy bank, my feet kept slipping off the wet, muddy wall under the water. Thankful to have reached the edge, I tried not to panic while trying to find a way to secure my feet so that I could push my body out of the water.

It took a few minutes and some pretty fervent prayer, but I kept digging my feet into the muddy wall until they were set enough for me to pull myself up the bank and out of the water. Whew!

Sometimes living with unexpected and unplanned situations can leave you feeling like you're fighting to get your feet on firm ground again. In this week's study, you saw the differences between Ruth and Naomi at the beginning of their journey back to Bethlehem as widows. They had no security for their future. However, Ruth dug her feet into faith while Naomi held on to her bitterness.

Whenever you feel like you're unsure of the future and it feels like you might fall apart, God wants to be your security when life gets slippery. Whether you're dealing with icy stares in an unstable relationship or the oil slickness of an unpredictable job situation, you're never dealing with those situations alone because God is active and near.

In Psalm 121, the author compares God's presence and power to the unpredictability of the other gods the Israelites foolishly followed. One of the most notable gods, Baal, needed to be awakened by his followers in order to be attentive to their needs. During a dramatic showdown on Mount Carmel, the prophet Elijah taunted Baal's prophets, imploring them to wake their sleeping god. Yet Elijah called upon the name of the Almighty God who demonstrated His power by sending down fire from heaven and settling the score between Elijah and the false prophets in an unforgettable way!

You never need to wonder if God is asleep or unavailable to help. Psalm 43:1 reminds us that God is ever-present in times of trouble. There will never, ever be an unexpected moment in your life when God isn't present and active in your life.

Prayer

God, I am so grateful that You never let me stumble, even when I have no idea what's happening in my life. I am grateful that You are always-present, all-knowing, and all-powerful. Thank You for the assurance and confidence that I never have to fear being left alone; in Jesus' name. Amen.

Prayer Journaling Prompts

As you reflect on this week's study of Ruth and the lessons that you've learned, what do you need to talk with God about today? Are you like Naomi and bitter about some area of your life that has "detoured in a ditch"?

Consider the lessons that you've learned about Ruth. What do you admire about her faithfulness and obedience?

As you write out your prayer today, what do you want to say to God about where you are in your waiting room journey? Confess the places where you've been bitter or angry about waiting and whether or not you recognize any steps of faith you need to take.

God, Now What?

We can choose to walk the better road
rather than the bitter road.

Welcome/Prayer/Icebreaker (5-10 minutes)

Welcome to Session 2 of I'm *Waiting, God*. This week we've considered what to do when unexpected events throw our lives off course. Today we're exploring what Ruth has to teach us about how to choose a better road rather than a bitter road. Take a moment to open with prayer, and then go around the circle and briefly describe a time when you had to embrace the unexpected when traveling.

Video (about 20 minutes)

Play the Group Centering video for Week 2 (optional), taking a couple of minutes to focus your hearts and minds on God and God's Word. Then play the video segment for Week 2, filling in the blanks as you watch and making notes about anything that resonates with you or that you want to be sure to remember.

—Video Notes—

Scriptures: Ruth 1:11-13, Ruth 1:16-17, Romans 12:12 (Our "Better Road" GPS), Ruth 2:11-12, Ruth 2:20, Ruth 4:14-16, Joel 2:25

_____, that's the story that blames God for the pain in our past.

_____ is the story that believes God will be faithful in our future.

Sometimes God's _____ gives us an opportunity to _____ our hearts.

The way we live with unanswered prayer is a powerful part of our _____.

Other Insights:

Group Discussion (20-25 minutes for a 60-minute session; 30-35 minutes for a 90-minute session)

Video Discussion

- What story have you been telling yourself about the unanswered prayers or unexpected changes in your life? Has your story been leading you down the road of better or bitter?
- How has unanswered prayer helped you examine your heart? What has it revealed about areas where you struggle to trust God?
- When and how has God brought purpose through pain in your life?
- What helps you to recognize God's blessings and remember His faithfulness?

Workbook Discussion

- Take turns reading Ruth 1:1-17 aloud. How would you tell this part of Ruth and Naomi's story in your own words? What do you learn from Ruth's spiritual declaration in these verses? (page 48)
- How would you describe the relationship between Ruth, Naomi, and Orpah? Do you have relationships like that in your life? If so, share about what they mean to you.
- *"When our prayers go unanswered, one of God's most beautiful blessings is someone who comforts us"* (page 46). When and how have you known the comfort of a friend or relative in a difficult season?
- *"Naomi's bitterness seems to come from the expectation that a powerful God could have stopped the pain and loss in her life. Since He didn't, Naomi is bitter"* (page 49). When have you found yourself feeling like Naomi, wondering why God didn't prevent a pain or loss? Have you had a season of bitterness toward God? If so, and if you're comfortable sharing, tell about that season and how you came through it.
- *"The way that you live with unanswered prayer is a powerful part of your testimony. A testimony isn't about living so that others are impressed; rather, a testimony is unspoken but action-based evidence of where and what you put your faith in"* (page 54). What did you discover about Ruth's testimony as she determined to take care of herself and her mother-in-law? What do you think of when you hear the word *testimony*? If you are in the midst of an unplanned or unexpected

detour in life and God hasn't answered your prayers, what kind of testimony might your life be speaking to the people around you? What are the words that you'd like to be attached to your testimony? (page 54)

- Who was Boaz? What is significant about his entrance into Ruth and Naomi's story? Are there people in your life who are like Boaz to you? (page 56) If so, share about them.
- When Naomi hears about Boaz, we see a subtle shift in her attitude toward God. She had been bitter, but now she is recognizing the kindness of God to her family. What do you think she was feeling as Ruth told her about Boaz? When and how has the kindness of God made a crack in a wall you built up around your heart?
- Read Ruth 3:1-12 aloud. What were the bold moves that Naomi told Ruth to take? What is the purpose of her plan? (page 58) Do you think you could have done what Ruth did? Why or why not? What bold moves of faith has God asked you to take previously? What bold move or step of faith is God calling you to take in this season of your life?
- "*Sometimes living with unexpected and unplanned situations can leave you feeling like you're fighting to get your feet on firm ground again*" (page 66). How can we grow in our faith and begin to trust the kindness of God, even when the ground beneath our feet feels shaky?

Learning to Wait (10-15 minutes – 90-minute session only)

Divide into groups of two or three and discuss the following (see page 63):

- What are one or two things that you've learned from Ruth's life this week?
- How is God prompting you to think or live differently as a result of what you've heard or learned this week?

Closing Prayer (5 minutes)

Close the session by sharing personal prayer requests and praying together. If you like, invite the women to surround those who have shared requests and pray for them aloud. In addition to praying aloud for one another, close by asking God to help you choose to travel the better road so that you may experience His blessings along the way.

Week 3

The Unnamed Bleeding Woman

Healing from the Inside Out

(Mark 5:24-34)

Memory Verse

When you go through deep waters,
I will be with you.
When you go through rivers of difficulty,
you will not drown.
When you walk through the fire of oppression,
you will not be burned up;
the flames will not consume you.

(Isaiah 43:2 NLT)

In her blockbuster hit "Blessings," Grammy-winning worship leader Laura Story bears her soul in a simple song that asks whether the hardest things that we face in life are actually blessings in disguise. In her book *When God Doesn't Fix It*, Laura explains her heart behind the song: "It is filled with questions I was asking in my personal life, with answers I wasn't sure I believed but hoped were true. It is a very personal and vulnerable song, filled with some hard theology."[1]

Shortly after their marriage, Laura's husband, Martin Elvington, was diagnosed with a brain tumor. After Martin's surgery, the doctors told Laura that her husband's long-term memory function was damaged. Grateful that Martin survived the surgery, she realized that her fairy-tale hopes of a happy life in marriage and ministry would never be.

Even though she prayed every day for God to heal Martin, Laura also learned how to trust God each day in absence of that healing. With frequent admissions of sadness, grief, and confusion, Laura struggled with a situation that God didn't fix. Over the years, she humbly accepted the journey that unfolded before her. In the process, Laura stepped forward with her story, even the hard parts, so that God could use not only her talents but even her ongoing struggles to help others.

There's a powerful, uncomfortable and complex truth that Laura shares in hopes of helping us understand the heart of God when we don't understand why God doesn't fix some of the problems in our lives: "Sometimes, God uses things he hates—things like cancer, divorce, suicide, addiction, death, and more—to accomplish the things he loves. He does this regularly and faithfully. It's only when we bring our pain to him that we can find our dwelling in him."[2]

It's important to recognize that God can use the things that He hates, but He doesn't create the situations that He hates. The consequences of human sin and a broken world create our pain and heartache, but God is powerful enough to restore, rebuild, and redeem all things. It's amazing how we can cry and celebrate God's blessing in our lives, even when He doesn't fix our situation. Even as Martin remains unhealed, Laura reminds us of hope that we find in Romans 8:28. She writes, "Even when we can't immediately see how our story fits into God's story of redemption, Scripture promises that it always does."[3]

If you're dealing with a place in life today and God hasn't fixed it, my heart is with you. A wise friend told me once, "If you feel like God is leading you to keeping praying for it, keep praying!" In time, God may fix it or He will give you the faith to live beyond it and bless you in other ways. I don't write that sentence lightly. Yet, even today I can see how God has used what He hates to accomplish something in my life that may not have been accomplished any other way.

This week's study is all about what happens when our waiting room months and weeks stretch into years of waiting. If you or someone you know has been praying for years and is still waiting for God to answer those prayers, there's hope and help waiting for you in the lessons that we're going to learn this week.

Day 1: When You Hurt for So Long

Gratitude Moment

Today I am grateful to God for _____

_____

_____

_____.

WAITING ROOM PROBLEM

In the face of pain and unanswered prayer, are you asking questions such as

Do I need more faith, or do I just need to try harder?

This week, we're leaping forward from Ruth's story over many centuries and multiple generations into the New Testament where Jesus heals a woman who's been suffering and struggling for many years. The specifics of her condition might create some awkward and uncomfortable feelings, especially if you grew up or interact with communities where people don't like to talk openly about embarrassing topics.

When your unanswered prayer is paired with secrecy and suffering, it can feel like too much! Not only do you feel the emptiness of the unanswered prayer; you also may feel like you're suffocating in secrecy because you're afraid or ashamed to talk about what you're going through with others.

Because we can't heal when we hide, the enemy loves it when we keep our pain and suffering a secret. So, when we feel embarrassed about our unanswered prayers in the sensitive areas of life such as singleness, marriage struggles, sexual struggles, self-harm, infertility, mental health, addiction, career failure, or financial crisis, he shows up in our shamed silence and whispers, You're all alone in this. You've been praying, but has God helped you? His whisper reinforces our embarrassment, and if we aren't fully equipped to fight in faith, we'll begin to wonder if it's our fault that God hasn't answered our prayer.

In my waiting journey, I've asked myself that question and God has used a long season of unanswered prayer to bless me with freedom from assuming that God is waiting for me to achieve a certain level of faith before He answers my prayer. I want you to experience that victory, too!

While our character this week has no name, I think that we can all relate to some aspect of her story. You may connect with the symbolism of her unnamed state, the duration of her suffering, or the dramatic encounter that she had with Jesus. No matter where you connect, know that just as Jesus showed up in the life of this hurting woman, so he's waiting to show up and make a difference in your life today, too.

Read Mark 5:21-25, and complete the following:

When Jesus crossed over the lake, a large _____ gathered around him.

A synagogue leader named _____ begged Jesus to come because the man's daughter was _____.

As Jesus went with Jairus, the large crowd followed, including a woman who had been bleeding for _____ years.

We meet this unnamed woman because she is part of a crowd following Jesus as he is on the way to the home of Jairus, one of the synagogue leaders, whose daughter is dying (Mark 5:23).

How does she end up in the crowd? While we don't know her name, she isn't alone in her interest in Jesus. In fact, Gospel writers make note on many occasions that large crowds often followed Jesus. People from all over Israel left their homes, jobs, and families to find Jesus. Here's what Mark wrote just a couple of chapters earlier:

> [7]Jesus withdrew with his disciples to the lake, and a large crowd from Galilee followed. [8]When they heard about all he was doing, many people came to him from Judea, Jerusalem, Idumea, and the regions across the Jordan and around Tyre and Sidon. [9]Because of the crowd he told his disciples to have a small boat ready for him, to keep the people from crowding him. [10]For he had healed many, so that those with diseases were pushing forward to touch him.

(Mark 3:7-10)

Fill in the blank below.

When people found out that Jesus was miraculously healing the sick, many people with diseases reached forward to _____ Jesus.

This was back before Jesus could "check in" his location like on social media and there was no Find Friends app, so the people had to follow the stories of Jesus' miracles and teachings until they found him. Turns out this would have been a powerful blessing! As they traveled to towns where Jesus had been, the newly healed and restored would tell their stories of encountering Jesus. Can you imagine the light in the eyes of all who testified to Jesus' healing power? Perhaps our unnamed woman was inspired by stories of those who'd come in contact with Jesus.

Whenever I hear or a read a story about how Jesus transformed a life, it adds fire to my spirit and energy to my soul. In her book A *Place of Healing*, Joni Eareckson Tada says it like this: "How else do you treat the subject of suffering? Sharing about suffering is like giving a blood transfusion...infusing powerful, life-transforming truths into the spiritual veins of another. And you can't do that with words only. Or, you shouldn't. How can you learn about suffering except by feeling the pain yourself."[4]

For the individuals who traveled to town after town in search of Jesus, the before-and-after transformation stories were enough to keep them pressing toward finding Jesus, even when their bodies ached in pain.

You don't need me to tell you that twelve years is a long time. It is! Just some basic math here: Unless ill or pregnant, the average woman has a monthly period for an average of 40 years of her life. This translates to 3,500 days. Since the unnamed woman has been bleeding every day for twelve years, that adds up to 4,380 days, which is 880 more days than the average woman over a lifetime! Take a moment and let that sink in.

Put a placeholder in Mark 5 and flip to Leviticus 15. Read verses 19-24 to learn more about how the unnamed woman would face each day with such a condition. List everyone and everything that would be unclean if she touches it during that time:

This all feels and sounds quite harsh, so let's look at what's going on from God's perspective. When you see words such as unclean, the word isn't attached to a person's human value in God's eyes; rather, unclean refers to the condition that must be dealt with to either restore a person or to protect the greater community. I've included an Extra Insight in the margin to help you understand the culture that our unnamed woman has lived in more fully.

Unfortunately, some of us grew up in homes where there was little to no talking about female development because of shame that has roots in the misunderstanding of God's instructions in Leviticus. But what if God gave those guidelines to protect women from exhaustion or inconsiderate mates? One source suggests, "Once again, God wasn't condemning or punishing the woman for experiencing her normal monthly period. . . . But this confinement was a blessing in disguise since it allowed her to enjoy rest and quiet when she needed it most."[6]

If you keep reading, Leviticus 15:25-33 explains what happens when a woman experiences ongoing bleeding. Essentially, a woman who continues to bleed beyond her monthly cycle will be unclean as long as she bleeds. So the unnamed woman who shows up in the crowd following Jesus has spent twelve years unable to be with her family, live in her home, or participate in the traditions of her faith because of her physical condition.

Considering her medical condition, describe what kind of quality of life the unnamed woman would have had.

When I think of her life before she came face-to-face with Jesus, words such as lonely, angry, frustrated, desperate, tired, and aching come to mind. Does she weep over memories of happier days when she had love, hope, and a family? Now, she is alone and no one can touch her without bringing inconvenience upon themselves. She cannot reach out for comfort or help, no matter how badly she wants it. Perhaps the unnamed woman repeats the words of David in Psalm 13:2: "How long must I struggle with anguish in my soul, / with sorrow in my heart every day?" (NLT).

We may not know the day-to-day pain of her life, but we get clues of the physical, social, and economic toll of her disease.

Extra Insight

"Leviticus also often uses the language of "unclean," "clean," and "holy" differently than today. With "unclean" and "clean," for example, most modern readers are tempted to think of that which is "non-hygienic" or "hygienic." In Leviticus, however, these words do not refer to hygiene at all. . . . Leviticus sets forth three basic ritual states: the unclean, the clean, and the holy. On the one hand, these categories guide the community with reference to the types of actions a person may (or may not) engage in, or the places that a person may (or may not) go.[5]

Read Mark 5:26. Write what you learn about her story in that verse:

She had visited many _____.

She had not gotten better, only _____.

She'd spent _____ that she had.

In just a short verse, we learn a lot about this unnamed woman. At first, we might celebrate that she had access to healthcare and that she had some wealth because only the wealthy could afford a physician. However, we read that she visited many doctors, spent all of her money, and still, her condition remained. In fact, it got worst. I'm not even sure how twelve years of nonstop bleeding can get worse, but right now, my heart goes out to her!

During that time, women who had prolonged menstrual cycles were subjected to all sorts of different "treatments." Here's an explanation of some of those treatments recorded in the Babylonian Talmud:

Let them procure three kapiza of Persian onions, boil them in wine, make her drink it, and say to her, "Cease your discharge." But if not, she should be made to sit at cross-roads, hold a cup of wine in her hand, and a man comes up from behind, frightens her and exclaims, "Cease your discharge!" But if not, a handful of cummin, a handful of saffron, and a handful of fenugreek are brought and boiled in wine, she is made to drink it and they say to her, "Cease your discharge." But, if not, let sixty pieces of sealing clay of a [wine] vessel be brought and let them smear her and say to her, "Cease your discharge."[7]

First, let us take a moment and give thanks that no one needs to walk behind us and scare the stuffing out of us when we've got a medical issue!

As outrageous as those treatments are, I spared you details about the final treatment that called for grain and animal dung. Women without any other options would agree to these treatments if it meant they had a chance to end their suffering and get their families back.

When we're facing long-term emotional, physical, or relational pain, it can literally feel like our lifeblood is being drained empty each day.

If your overall physical and emotional wellness looked like a gas gauge, where would you be right now? Circle the appropriate line at the top of the following page:

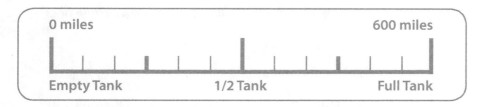

0 miles   600 miles

Empty Tank   1/2 Tank   Full Tank

What circumstances are draining your tank each day? How long have you been feeling drained?

How have your long-term pain and suffering drawn you closer to God or pushed you away from God?

Whether your struggle is days old or decades long, I want God's words to you to have the last word in our time together today. While I love you as a spiritual sister in Christ, I know that only God can soothe the ache in your soul. So if you feel drained, dried up, or desperate, open your heart and pour in God's promises to fill your soul. You might not feel them at first, but keep your heart open and keep pouring.

Memory Verse Reflection

Isaiah 43:2 (NLT) is a beautiful message of hope from God to the Israelites, who had been suffering in captivity for many years. Here's what God said to them:

When you go through deep waters,
*   I will be with you.*
When you go through rivers of difficulty,
*   you will not drown.*
When you walk through the fire of oppression,
*   you will not be burned up;*
*   the flames will not consume you.*

What do you feel best describes your life right now? Circle one:

a. Deep waters – feeling overwhelmed

b. Rivers of difficulty – obstacles everywhere

c. Fire of oppression – heartache and hardships that aren't your fault

When you read this verse, how does God's promise that He will be with you encourage you today?

I read this verse pretty often. From personal experience, I know the pain of deep waters, rivers of difficulty, and the fire of oppression. But this is not the only time when God speaks words of encouragement over us. The Bible is filled with God's promises to be with us no matter what we are facing!

Prayer

Dear God, You are with me today in my ache and my pain. I need the comfort that only You can provide to soothe the pain in my heart and soul; in Jesus' name. Amen.

Day 2: Using the Faith that You Have

WAITING ROOM PRINCIPLE

When you're hurting and suffering, fight to get to Jesus!

During those early years of our family crisis, I lived a lot like the unnamed bleeding woman did before she went looking for Jesus. I went into full crisis-mode. Like her, I spent years and a lot of money talking with medical professionals and counselors and reading books. I kept thinking that if I tried harder, eventually I could figure out a fix for our painful situation.

However, nothing worked. After a few disastrous attempts to force solutions, I had to admit that I was powerless over what was happening. That was hard. But I was more willing to pray and started attending a recovery group to get the help that I needed. It was God's mercy that sustained my broken heart as our family situation grew worse. Compounding the years of tears were the well-meaning comments from a few folks who asked, "Are you sure that you're praying hard enough?" While I know that those comments were spoken from a place of love and concern, it felt like hot judgment heaped upon my hurting heart. Even though God's truth kept the hurtful comments from taking root in my heart, the judgment still stung.

If you've been in a long season of unanswered prayer and you haven't reached out to ask for professional help or medical intervention, I want to give you permission to make that call today! There's nothing wrong with asking for help, but don't put your faith and trust in medical advice or human wisdom. Ask others for help, but put your faith in God.

So, what do you do when you've done all that you can do and nothing changes? Is it a matter of not having enough faith?

As the unnamed bleeding woman meets Jesus face-to-face, she shows us that it's not about the amount of faith you have; it's where you direct the faith that you do have.

Read Mark 5:27-28 in the margin. What is her goal?

27When she heard about Jesus, she came up behind him in the crowd and touched his cloak,28because she thought, "If I just touch his clothes, I will be healed."
(Mark 5:27-28)

Our unnamed friend doesn't know all that we know now about Jesus—about His sacrifice for us on the cross and the scope of His love and grace. She has heard that Jesus raises people from the dead and heals them. That is all that she needs to know, and she goes straight for Jesus.

She doesn't question whether or not she has enough faith.
She doesn't aim to ask for a favor.
She isn't going to bargain with Jesus or try to pay Him off.
Step-by-step, she inches her way to Jesus with her hand outstretched.
Our unnamed friend has quite a fight in front of her. Consider the urgency and the desperation of the crowd. Everyone needs help, including those who are a little stronger and less sick. After twelve years of blood loss, she is likely weak. I can picture her wincing in pain as she bumps against the other bodies. Does she think about giving up when she's pushed back and shoved around? I wonder how she battles the ingrained levitical rule that she shouldn't touch a man when she is bleeding. No matter how she feels, this unnamed woman is a warrior

fighting forward. She fights her way inch-by-inch to Jesus. A strong resolve sustains a weak body. There's an important lesson in that for us.

When you get tired, especially when you're not feeling well, the temptation is to think you need to take a break from the very things that will build you back up such as prayer, Bible study, and community. But when life hurts, that is exactly the time when you need help the most. However, seeking help doesn't come easy—not because Jesus isn't waiting for you, but because you might decide not to show up. Sometimes the weight of waiting drains our energy and we just don't feel like doing anything—even the things that will make us feel better, such as reading a devotional, taking a walk, praying, or going to church.

Here's the truth, my friend: Jesus is always waiting for you.

So, if you've been far from Jesus because you've been out looking for other solutions, remember that Jesus is waiting for you. And if you feel far from Jesus because you're in so much pain that you don't think you can go on, He will come right to you. It's okay if you have to fight through your feelings, busy schedule, aches, pains, and judgmental people; but never let anything stop you from getting close to Jesus!

As one who understands Jewish law, Jesus knows that many of the sick hands reaching for him belong to people who have been declared unclean. As they touch Jesus, he will become unclean as well. Religious leaders watching would have been offended and incensed that Jesus, a rabbi, would allow sick people to get so close.

Jesus allowing the crowds of sick people to swarm him is a powerful illustration of how we're all spiritually sick with sin, yet Jesus invites us all to come to Him. He would even go to the cross to take on our spiritual sickness so that we can experience eternal life with God.

Matthew and Luke also report the unnamed bleeding woman's story, but they devote only a couple of verses to her. Still, both of these accounts identify the specific part of Jesus' robe that she touched:

> She touched the **fringe** of his robe.
> (*Matthew 9:20 NLT, emphasis added*)

> Coming up behind Jesus, she touched the **fringe** of his robe.
> (*Luke 8:44 NLT, emphasis added*)

Like other Jews, Jesus would be wearing tassels on the corner of his outer robe. In Numbers 15:38-40, God told Moses to instruct the people to attach the tassels with blue cords. Those tassels were to remind the Israelites to obey God's commandments and to live as God's holy and

chosen people. There were some who believed that the fringe on the cloak of anyone in holy service to God had healing qualities.

The woman's goal is just to touch Jesus' clothing. Whether or not she is specifically reaching for his tassels, it is unclear. Could this be because there is a lot of competition for the other parts of Jesus' person? All we know is that when she makes contact with Jesus' clothing, her life immediately changes.

Read Mark 5:29-31, and answer the questions below.

How quickly does her bleeding stop?

How does the woman feel in her body?

What does Jesus notice in that moment?

Instantly, the unnamed bleeding woman is healed. While she isn't the only person recorded in the Gospel of Mark to be healed after touching the fringe on Jesus' clothes (see Mark 6:56 in the margin), this is the only place where we read that Jesus senses when healing power goes out from him.[8]

As the woman recognizes her healing, Jesus turns and begins to look around the crowd.

What question does Jesus ask the crowd?

Why do the disciples sound so puzzled at Jesus' question?

Wherever he went— in villages, cities, or the countryside— they brought the sick out to the marketplaces. They begged him to let the sick touch at least the fringe of his robe, and all who touched him were healed.
(Mark 6:56 NLT)

As the disciples are looking around at the pressing crowd, it would be impossible to tell the difference between who is trying to touch Jesus and those who are bumping or shoving into him.

But Jesus knows.

He knows exactly who has touched him in faith before she ever speaks up. He knows her story. He knows her struggle. Most of all, Jesus knows her shame and suffering. She is healed just as she is. Ancient theologian Augustine offers this observation about Jesus' foreknowledge of the unnamed woman: "'Flesh presses, faith touches.'... He can always distinguish between the jostle of a curious mob, and the agonized touch of a needy soul." [9]

Does Jesus answer this woman's prayer because she has super-size faith, or is it because she directs whatever faith she does have solely toward Him?

You're not alone if you've wondered if you need to do more to grow your faith so that God might answer your prayer. This is a nuanced area of discussion, so let's walk through it with Scripture, beginning with a request that Jesus' disciples make in Luke 17:5-6 (NLT):

The apostles said to the Lord, "Show us how to increase our faith."

The Lord answered, "If you had faith even as small as a mustard seed, you could say to this mulberry tree, 'May you be uprooted and be planted in the sea,' and it would obey you!"

A mustard seed is very small. A mulberry tree has a dense root system, enabling it to live a long life. Transplanting a mulberry tree with such a root system would be very difficult, and it would be next to impossible to replant the tree in the ocean. So, Jesus is saying that even small faith can cause seemingly impossible things to happen. [10]

Extra Insight

"The faith that we must have is a faith that has more to do with what *kind* of faith it is than with *how much* faith there is."
—David Guzik [11]

This is beautiful news for each of us, especially if our faith feels battered and worn down by long-time struggling or suffering while waiting for an answer to prayer. You might be thinking that God no longer hears your prayers because you have so little faith. The good news is that you only need a little faith today! What's more important than the amount of your faith is the object of your faith!

When we're focused on how much faith we have, that's when we're trying to do what we hope will stack up favor with God. However, the accumulation of our faith should enlarge our view of God and His power, not become chips that we hope to use in bargaining for an answered prayer.

Just to make sure that you and I are still on the same page, let me summarize a few key thoughts:

1. You don't have to keep doing more for God to answer your prayers.
2. The smallest amount of faith in God can accomplish miracles.

3. We grow in faith to experience a greater understanding of God, not to increase our expectations of what God will do for us.

Considering Jesus' response to his disciples' request in Luke 17 prompted me to stop and think about why I do the things that I do in my Christian life. So, here's what it looks like in life when I get stuck in what I'm calling "Try-harder" faith versus the times when I rest in having "Mustard-seed" faith:

Put a checkmark beside those statements or questions that tend to show up in your life most often?

"Try-harder" Faith	*"Mustard-seed" Faith*
Am I praying enough?	God, I desire Your presence more than I ask You to solve my problems.
Did I read my Bible today?	God, I want to know more about You, Your character, and what it means to experience life with You.
Am I volunteering/serving enough?	God, do I love others as You love me?
How much do I need to give this week?	God, thank You for Your generosity to me! Everything I have is Yours!

When do you feel the "try harder" temptation the most?

How does mustard-seed faith free us from the stress of trying to please God?

If you drift toward the "try harder" camp as I do, then perhaps you might consider wisdom from pastor and author John Ortberg as he invites us to "try softer":

> Trying softer means focusing more on God's goodness than our efforts. It means being more relaxed and self-conscious. Less pressured. When I try softer, I am less defensive, more open to feedback. I learn better. I stay patient if things don't turn out the way I expected.[12]

As I discussed the concept of try-softer with the women in my pilot group while writing the study, my friend Ann remarked, "When I try softer, I'm more open-handed, feel less panicked, and do much better."

When you think about today's Waiting Room Principle of not letting anything keep you from reaching out to Jesus, consider where your "try harder" tendencies might be getting in your way. Maybe you don't struggle with "try harder" but are just tired. You're worn out from all the years of waiting and struggle. Be encouraged today that you only need to have a little faith focused on a big God for something miraculous to happen.

Today's Takeaway

The amount of faith that I have isn't as important as Who my faith is in.

Prayer

Dear God, thank You that Your love for us isn't based on our goodness or good deeds. I am so grateful that just as Jesus invited the crowds to come near with their sickness and pain, You have invited me to find eternal healing in You through the free gift of salvation in Jesus Christ.

God, help me to live in the truth that I don't need to try harder to get You to answer my prayers; rather, I simply need to focus my faith on You and trust that You will answer my prayer in the way that is best for me. Give me the faith I need to accept that; in Jesus' name. Amen.

Day 3: Enjoying the Blessing

Read Mark 3:30-33, and answer the following questions.

When Jesus asks who touched him, how does the woman react?

Why is she so afraid?

What does she do after falling at Jesus' feet?

Gratitude Moment

Today I am grateful to God for _____

_____

_____

_____

_____.

Yesterday, we discussed that Jesus knows exactly who has touched Him. Now, imagine that you're this woman. After over a decade of constant bleeding, you're instantly healed. The feeling of life draining from your body is gone. Having suffered for so many years, you're used to the feeling of barely making it through every day. Your normal is barely feeling alive, and now you are healed. How do you think you would react?

She must be freaked out!

Now Jesus wants her to speak up. That must flip her out even more! Not only is she still trying to figure out how the power of Christ has healed her, she also knows that she has to admit reaching out and touching Jesus in her unclean state. Even though there are lots of unclean people in the crowd, for her to admit touching Jesus and making Him unclean could result in punishment from the religious leaders in the crowd. Yet the woman is grateful enough and brave enough to come forward and tell Jesus the "whole truth" (Mark 5:33) about who she is and what she has done.

Is there something that keeps you from telling the "whole truth" about some area of your life? Is there a confession that you are holding back from God or others because of fear or condemnation?

If you have told God or others the "whole truth," how have you sensed or experienced freedom?

Are there any places where you're still trying to navigate the consequences of telling the "whole truth"? Where do you need to trust God in this?

I want to remind you that on these pages and in this moment, you've come into a "grace space." You are free to tell the whole truth. If you don't want to write in this workbook because you are afraid someone might see it, then get a separate sheet of paper to answer these important questions. In this moment, you have permission to push back against the enemy's doomsday whisper and be real about anything you've been holding back. You cannot heal until you reveal the truth. Not sure where to begin? Start with telling Jesus the whole truth! You can talk to Him about it right now. You can pray aloud or, if the words are too hard to say, you can write a letter to Jesus.

Romans 8:1 reminds us that we never have to fear condemnation from God, even when we struggle. Though it is true that people may say hurtful or judgmental things to you, that's different from how God sees you and your situation.

It's only when you fight your fear and come face-to-face with Jesus that you realize no condemnation is waiting for you. Only love and peace.

What's next? James 5:16 tells us that we must confess our sins and struggles to others so that we can find healing. Stay with me! God gives us other people to hold us up while He heals us. The healing journey is often a long process and we need the loving support of those who will pray for us, point us to Jesus, and love us through our struggle toward spiritual freedom, victory, or health.

If you are looking for safe places to speak the truth, I urge you to seek out safe people. For the most sensitive and potentially dangerous situations, I strongly recommend talking with your medical professional or a licensed counselor. For other sensitive issues, confide in a safe person. (I've identified some qualities of safe people in the margin.) If you need words to start the conversation, you can use these: "There's something very difficult that I need to talk about. I feel scared, awkward, and ashamed right now. I want to tell someone about what is going on in my life. But I want to make sure that my situation will not be shared and I will not be shamed for speaking up."

As one who has had to speak up about embarrassing, unanswered prayer as well as sit across from women in the same situation, I want you

to know that there are safe places for you to talk about what's going on. Don't let anyone, including the enemy of your soul, convince you that there are not!

> **Read Mark 5:34 and write out the verse below. Circle the words "Daughter" and "peace."**

Notice how Jesus begins with "Daughter," a lovely term of belonging and endearment. At His first word, the unnamed bleeding woman knows that Jesus isn't condemning or being critical of her actions. Can you see her lifting her head and looking into his eyes upon hearing such a word after years of isolation? It has been years since she has been spoken to with such love and kindness. But Jesus doesn't stop there!

As she sits before him with the crowd gathered around, Jesus speaks the words "your faith has healed you." The Hebrew word for "healed" is *sózó*, which means "saved" or "healed."[13] So more than just a physical healing, this woman has experienced a spiritual healing, too. This is so important to celebrate because it would be a tragedy for her to experience physical healing but continue to live with a suffering mindset. Perhaps you know someone who has survived cancer, made it through a bitter divorce, stopped taking drugs, or found a job after years of unemployment, and yet she continues to suffer emotionally and mentally. Our spiritual healing is even more important than our physical healing!

> **Consider your situation. Imagine that God has answered your long-awaited prayer and you finally have received what you really want. Why would you still need to pursue emotional and spiritual healing?**

One of the sweetest parts of this entire dialogue is that Jesus affirms the woman in the presence of others. He doesn't take her aside for their conversation. No, instead he speaks of her faith aloud, restoring her dignity. Surely this would bless her because she likely has heard years'

Identifying a Safe Person

In my experience as a long-time church leader and former professional life coach, there are three important recommendations when searching for a safe person to talk to:

1. Seek recommendations from your pastor or your Bible study leader (if she isn't available to sit down and talk with you).

2. Choose someone of the same sex as you to protect yourself from unintended or inappropriate emotional bonding that may result from highly vulnerable conversations.

3. Choose someone who can support and invest in you afterward by checking in by text or phone call to see how you're doing.

worth of whispers from people in her community who wonder what secret sin must have kept her from healing. Right there in public, Jesus affirms that she doesn't need to be a spiritual giant to receive her inside-out healing; rather, he applauds her steadfast, focused faith in Him.

Jesus' final words to the woman are "Go in peace...." The Hebrew word for "peace" in this verse is *eiréné* and means "peace of mind."[14] There is nothing like the peace of mind that only God can provide.

Because she is healed, the unnamed woman has to travel to her home and rebuild her life. Even after her body is healed, she still is going to have problems and difficulties; but with the blessing of peace of mind, she will be able to face all that is in front of her.

Why is peace of mind such a blessing?

How do you know when you're experiencing the peace of mind that only God can provide?

We don't know what happens in her life after she returns home. My hope is that she continued to testify to Jesus' healing touch and lived faithfully. But not everyone Jesus heals stops to testify. Shortly after the disciples ask Jesus to increase their faith, Jesus heals ten lepers who cry out for help, but only one comes back to thank Him (Luke 17:11-19).

There are many times in life when God does answer our prayers and provides that much-desired job, rescues the rebellious child, restores health, or rebuilds the broken marriage.

Can you recall a time when God specifically answered a long-awaited prayer? If so, describe it briefly:

In my life, there are so many examples, such as a miraculous solution to funding my girls' Christian education, my full-time job at the church, an opportunity to go into full-time women's ministry, and so many more. Recently, my youngest daughter and I were praying for funds

to buy her a car. A few months later, she was gifted a car by a group of people who were so proud of how she handled our family's adversity and who wanted to bless her. I was blown away!

However, when God does give us our heart's desire, He doesn't want us to forget about the path that we've followed and what we've learned in the seasons of unanswered prayer.

In Deuteronomy, God instructs Moses to teach the people everything they need to know to set up their new lives in the Promised Land, and that instruction includes a reminder and warning.

Read Deuteronomy 8:12-14 in the margin.

Even though God writes this message specifically to the Israelites, what lesson can you draw from it for your life?

How can you continue to show God gratitude once your prayer has been answered, whether you've received what you hoped for or not?

¹²When you have become full and prosperous and have built fine homes to live in, ¹³and when your flocks and herds have become very large and your silver and gold have multiplied along with everything else, be careful! ¹⁴Do not become proud at that time and forget the LORD your God, who rescued you from slavery in the land of Egypt.

(Deuteronomy 8:12-14 NLT)

I have included the daily gratitude exercise in this study because giving thanks to God is powerful in seasons of unanswered prayer as well as in seasons of prosperity or times when life is going well. Remember, God's goodness when waiting for an answer to prayer reminds us of God's previous faithfulness. When you thank God when times are good, it's an act of humility that reminds you where your blessings come from. When you take time to give thanks, that expression of gratitude inches you toward Jesus.

Another way that I inch toward Jesus each day is reading Bible verses about God's promises for me and repeating them to myself. Since thousands of thoughts that I have each day tend to put distance between me and God, I must incorporate a strategic and effective tool to inch my heart and mind back to God. I turned this practice into an exercise that I call the God-Morning/God-Night Technique that first appeared in my *Winning the Worry Battle* book.

To start, I choose five Bible verses and write them on a notecard. Then, I post that notecard in my bathroom so that I can read the verses each morning and each night when I brush my teeth. Since I like having healthy teeth, I'm unlikely to miss brushing my teeth, which means that I'm unlikely to miss an opportunity to engage with God's promises to me.

There are so many promises in the Bible that you can choose if you'd like to do this. I've made a short list below that you can use to get started.

Seek the Kingdom of God above all else, and live righteously, and he will give you everything you need.

(Matthew 6:33 NLT)

Give all your worries and cares to God, for he cares about you.
(1 Peter 5:7 NLT)

For God has not given us a spirit of fear and timidity, but of power, love, and self-discipline.

(2 Timothy 1:7 NLT)

"Be strong and courageous! Do not be afraid or discouraged for the LORD your God is with you wherever you go."

(Joshua 1:9 NLT)

*The LORD is my strength and my song;
    he has given me victory.*
(Psalm 118:14 NLT)

WAITING ROOM APPLICATION

When you feel far away from Jesus, inch your way back to Him by giving thanks and recalling God's promises.

Today's Takeaway

It doesn't matter how fast or slow you move toward Jesus; it only matters that you do.

Prayer

Dear God, thank You for peace of mind! God, I am so grateful that You are the One who gives me the peace that passes all earthy understanding when I trust in You (Philippians 4:6-7). Even as I reflect on my waiting room situation, I may not know how long it will last but I do know that I can trust You with the outcome, which will be the greatest blessing to me. I am grateful for that; in Jesus' name. Amen.

Bible Story Wrap-Up

If you or someone that you know has been praying a long time for a breakthrough, a renew, or a rescue, I hope that your time with the unnamed bleeding woman's story poured fresh hope into your heart. If you feel that a circumstance in your life is draining your energy, reach out to Jesus. If you haven't shared your situation with a trusted friend, I implore you to do that as soon as you can!

Finally, if what you've been praying for has happened, don't forget about how God has sustained and cared for you while you waited. It's really easy to get focused on enjoying our blessing and forget about the One who loves to bless us. Keep giving thanks to God!

Now that we have come to the end of the unnamed bleeding woman's story, take a moment to consider what you have learned and how God is calling you to respond.

> What are one or two things that you've learned from the unnamed bleeding woman's life this week?

> How is God prompting you to think or live differently as a result of what you've heard or learned this week?

Day 4: Self-Study (*Optional*)

Today you have the opportunity to participate in an optional self-study with a Bible verse or passage of your choosing. The Verse Bank on page 145 features Scriptures that fit thematically with the unnamed bleeding woman. Select one of the Scriptures listed and follow these prompts.

Read

Write below the verse or passage you selected:

Reflect

Now open your Bible and read a few verses that precede and follow your chosen Scripture in order to gather a bigger picture of what is going on. Use study helps as needed or desired to answer questions such as these: Who is speaking? Who is the audience? When or where were these words written? What is the overarching message? Are there any words that you need to look up for better understanding? (Check out Bible search websites such as BibleGateway.com and others for commentaries, Bible dictionaries, and other tools.) Write your responses below.

Respond

Ask yourself the question: How does God want me to think or live differently as a result of what I've read? Consider how you can apply this passage to your life.

```



```

Release

Write a prayer to God expressing that you are willing to apply what you've learned to your life.

```



```

Day 5: Devotional and Prayer Journaling (*Optional*)

For our light and momentary troubles are achieving for us an eternal glory that far outweighs them all.

(2 Corinthians 4:17)

When my daughters were preschool age, they loved to ask, "Mommy, are we there yet?" every few minutes whenever we'd take a trip. Back then, cars didn't have DVD players or smartphones with YouTube. With little to distract them, every mile felt like an eternity even though we were only driving an hour or two to visit their grandparents.

During certain long and difficult seasons of life, my journals are filled with phrases such as "How long, God?" or "When will this be over?" Every hard day felt like a year, and some years felt like an eternity. If you're facing a chronic situation like the unnamed bleeding woman

Gratitude Moment

Today I am grateful to God for _____

_____

_____

_____

_____.

or a permanent hardship such as a permanent disability or a parent's dementia diagnosis, thinking about each day can be quite overwhelming.

How can we live so that our situation doesn't seem bigger than God? How can changing our perspective bless us and encourage us in an ongoing hard situation?

The apostle Paul provides just the wisdom we need. However, at first glance, we might be offended. How dare he describe our cancer diagnosis or financial crisis as "light and momentary"? Is Paul minimizing the heartache or chronic hardships that we're facing in life? Not at all! Rather, he invites us to stop seeing our life circumstances on a human time line of seventy or eighty years. Instead, we are to see the events of our lives in light of God's eternal timeline, which stretches into eternity. As believers who will experience life eternal with God, one day we're going to look back at our cancer battle, chronic illness, or difficult marriage and it will only be a blip on God's time line. It's hard to imagine that, but it's true.

I've tried to capture the two different perspectives in the drawings below. The top picture shows a long season of unanswered prayer. When we look at that long waiting room, it feels like a large chunk of life has been spent waiting on God.

However, that same long season in human years barely registers on the eternal time line, as noted by the tiny arrow in the second picture below. While it's hard to convey an accurate perspective on an eternal time line, I hope the distinction in perception has been made.

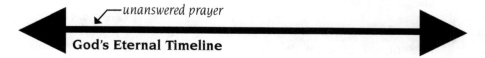

This was hard for me to do, especially during hard seasons when every day felt like an eternity. But then I read about Paul's life in 2 Corinthians 11:24-28 as he describes being beaten, stoned, shipwrecked three times, imprisoned, and constantly in danger. After all of that, how could Paul possibly describe his troubles and ours as "light and momentary"? It's because Paul learned to find the blessings of living according to God's eternal time line.

While our natural human response is to escape hardship and heartache as quickly as possible, Paul realized that every hard moment he lived through was an offering that gave glory to God. Every day that he spent in prison or shipwrecked on an island was a day when he could store up treasures in heaven by either sharing the gospel with others or simply trusting God for another day.

Paul never minimizes struggles, and you don't have to either. Even as he was upfront about the difficulties that he faced, you can be honest about the hard times and tough days. However, can you shift your perspective from seeing your struggle to looking for what God is producing in your life as a result of your struggle?

Could it be that whatever you can't change is what God is using not only to bring Him glory but also to bless your life?

Prayer

God, it's hard to stop focusing on my problems and fix my eyes on You. Help me change my perspective so that I can see Your eternal glory in my circumstances; in Jesus' name. Amen.

Prayer Journaling Prompts

As you reflect on this week's study on the unnamed bleeding woman and the lessons that you've learned, what do you need to talk about with God today? Consider the lessons that you've learned about the unnamed bleeding woman's encounter with Jesus. What has she taught you about having faith in Jesus instead of putting your faith in other solutions? How did the idea of "trying softer" versus "trying harder" settle into your heart and mind? What do you think God is calling you to do differently as a result?

As you write out your prayer today, talk to God honestly about where you're feeling drained and exhausted in your waiting room journey. Make note of any blessings that you experienced while doing this week's study and whether you recognize any steps of faith you need to take.

The Unnamed Bleeding Woman

Healing from the Inside Out

Jesus is enough when we're weary of waiting.

Welcome/Prayer/Icebreaker (5-10 minutes)

Welcome to Session 3 of I'm Waiting, God. This week we've considered how God can redeem and restore all things—even when He doesn't fix our situation. Today we're exploring what the unnamed bleeding woman has to teach us about reaching out to Jesus with whatever faith we have. Take a moment to open with prayer, and then go around the circle and share something that makes you tired—perhaps even just thinking about it!

Video (about 20 minutes)

Play the Group Centering video for Week 3 (optional), taking a couple of minutes to focus your hearts and minds on God and God's Word. Then play the video segment for Week 3, filling in the blanks as you watch and making notes about anything that resonates with you or that you want to be sure to remember.

—Video Notes—

Scripture: Mark 5:26, Mark 5:27-29, Luke 17:5-6

_____ is a pathway to Jesus.

Slowing down means _____ _____ of ourselves.

Jesus is _____ when we're weary of waiting.

Other Insights:

Group Discussion (20-25 minutes for a 60-minute session; 30-35 minutes for a 90-minute session)

Video Discussion

- How does the weight of waiting make us weary and even desperate?
- How can weakness or desperation move us toward Jesus?
- How can slowing down help us in times of waiting? What are some life-giving practices that can help sustain us?
- Have you ever felt that your unanswered prayers have to do with the amount of your faith? What does it mean to say that it's not the amount of our faith but the object of our faith that matters?

Workbook Discussion

- "When we feel embarrassed about our unanswered prayers in the sensitive areas of life such as singleness, marriage struggles, sexual struggles, self-harm, infertility, mental health, addiction, career failure, or financial crisis, [the enemy] shows up in our shamed silence and whispers. You're all alone in this. You've been praying, but has God helped you? His whisper reinforces our embarrassment, and if we aren't fully equipped to fight in faith, we'll begin to wonder if it's our fault that God hasn't answered our prayer" (pages 76–77). When have you heard the lies of the enemy telling you that you were alone in your struggle or waiting?
- Read Mark 5:21-28 aloud. Where is Jesus heading? Who does he encounter along the way?
- What did you learn about the woman who had been bleeding? Considering her medical condition, describe what kind of quality of life the unnamed woman would have had. (page 79)
- The woman was determined to get to Jesus after having exhausted all of her medical options. When have you been desperate to get to Jesus, knowing full well that He was your only hope?
- How have your long-term pain and suffering drawn you closer to God or pushed you away from God? (page 81)

- Read Isaiah 43:2 aloud. What is the hope in this verse? How does it encourage you today? (page 82)
- *"When you get tired, especially when you're not feeling well, the temptation is to think you need to take a break from the very things that will build you back up such as prayer, Bible study, and community. But when life hurts, that is exactly the time when you need help the most"* (page 84). Have you known this to be true in your life? If so, share about that time.
- Read Mark 5:29-34 aloud. Describe the scene in your own words. What do you think the woman felt? What do you think Jesus felt?
- How does mustard-seed faith free us from the stress of trying to please God? (page 87)
- *"At His first word, the unnamed bleeding woman knows that Jesus isn't condemning or being critical of her actions. Can you see her lifting her head and looking into his eyes upon hearing such a word after years of isolation?"* (page 91) When has the kindness of God caused you to lift your head from your situation to see God?
- *"More than just a physical healing, this woman has experienced a spiritual healing, too. This is so important to celebrate because it would be a tragedy for her to experience physical healing but continue to live with a suffering mindset"* (page 91). What does it mean to have a suffering mindset? Why do we need to pursue emotional and spiritual healing as well as physical? (see page 91)
- Jesus spoke a blessing of peace to the woman. Why is peace of mind such a blessing? How do you know when you're experiencing the peace of mind that only God can provide? (page 92) When have you known that kind of peace?

Learning to Wait (10-15 minutes – 90-minute session only)

Divide into groups of two or three and discuss the following (see page 95):

- What are one or two things that you've learned from the unnamed bleeding woman's life this week?
- How is God prompting you to think or live differently as a result of what you've heard or learned this week?

Closing Prayer (5 minutes)

Close the session by sharing personal prayer requests and praying together. If you like, invite the women to surround those who have shared requests and pray for them aloud. In addition to praying aloud for one another, close by asking God to help us see our weakness as a pathway to Him and allow Him to heal our suffering even if our situation doesn't change.

Week 4

Martha

Embracing the Better Blessing

(John 11)

Memory Verse

"He will wipe every tear from their eyes. There will be no more death or mourning or crying or pain, for the old order of things has passed away."

(Revelation 21:4)

On the warm summer day that young Cherise married her husband, she never thought that her marriage would end. The early years of their lives headed solidly in the direction of happily ever after. They graduated from college, had kids, bought a home, and found a church. Life wasn't perfect, but they laughed together every day and loved each other through mistakes.

Cherise's faith was always an important part of her life. But her good life and busy schedule made it tough for her to squeeze in time with God. Yet, she persisted. In the early mornings she would sneak into the spare bedroom of her five-bedroom home to study her Bible and pray. Back then, she started the habit of praying John the Baptist's well-known words: "He must increase, but I must decrease" (John 3:30 KJV).

As Cherise looks back, she can't put her finger on when their lives changed and the marriage crisis began. Even as she and her husband went on date nights and called each other each day, there were some troubling changes. Cherise realized that there were secrets being kept from her and unexplained behaviors causing more arguments. She spent many sleepless nights trying to figure out what was going wrong. Did something happen during a particular fight? Did I do something wrong?

Most of her prayers during that time were simple, "God, please help!" or "God, please fix this!" No matter whatever she tried, a hidden addiction made itself known in difficult and heart-breaking ways. Their first marriage separation happened right before their twentieth anniversary, followed by a second separation four years later.

During the second separation, a deeply depressed Cherise realized that she had to stop begging God to give back her good life and, instead, listen for His guidance to live the life in front of her. While she never audibly heard God's voice, Cherise realized that God was teaching her to live for His glory in the midst of her difficult circumstance. Although Cherise continued to pray for her marriage, a few years later her husband decided that he no longer wanted to be married. She was devastated but realized that God had blessed her years before by drawing her in close so that she discovered the blessing of His presence. That blessing sustained Cherise through an unanswered prayer that eventually turned into a heartbreaking "no."

Stories like Cherise's aren't easy to read. You may know from experience that these stories aren't easy to live, either.

In our idealized version of Christianity, we like to think that we pray, God answers, and we live happily ever after. However, cemeteries are a reminder that God never wants us to dream of happily ever after while we're living on earth because our broken, fallen world will rob us of that dream one way or another. Sometimes our waiting rooms and unexpected journeys are a setup for the better blessing that God wants to give us when He doesn't give us what we want.

Day 1: Waiting for Jesus

Gratitude Moment

Today I am grateful to God for _____

_____

_____

_____

_____ .

WAITING ROOM PROBLEM

How do you find hope when God doesn't give you what you've been waiting for?

This week we are exploring where to experience God's hope and blessing when it seems like our waiting room journey ends with a no. How do we live when God doesn't give us what we've been waiting for? This is a question that we're afraid to acknowledge out of fear that it might actually happen.

- What if God doesn't provide the needed funds before I lose my home?
- What if God doesn't change my spouse's heart before the divorce is finalized?
- What if God doesn't heal my cancer before the medicine stops working?
- What if God doesn't rescue my son or daughter before they overdose?
- What if God doesn't give me a baby or spouse before I get too old?

Often, we feel like we're racing against the clock in our waiting room journeys. A few years ago some coworkers and I participated in a fantasy

adventure game. We were blindfolded and taken into a locked room where we were told that we were fake prisoners on a fake island and that we had to work together on a variety of challenges and problems to solve a riddle to unlock the escape hatch. We had ninety minutes to break out, and we cheered when we escaped with only seconds to spare.

Do you feel like you're on the last few seconds of whatever you've been waiting for God to show up and save you from? Do you feel like time has run out and you're trying to deal with an unanswered prayer that looks like a "no"?

In this week's study, you're going to meet Martha. You might know some of her story from Luke 10. Martha is often remembered for her gift of hospitality and her open hostility at her sister for not helping with the chores. While different perspectives on Martha's life draw different conclusions, you'll discover that Martha as well as her siblings, Mary and Lazarus, are good friends of Jesus. Yet not even friendship can prevent the tragedy that is about to unfold. In this week's story, you will watch Martha grapple with Jesus' timing.

As we discover some unique lessons and insights, we will learn that God's timing doesn't always makes sense but is always for our eternal blessing and benefit.

Read John 11:1-12. Then draw a line to from the first column to the correct answer in the second column.

Lazarus was . . .   . . . in Bethany.

The disciples   . . . the disciples didn't realize
objected because . . .   that Lazarus had died.

Even after hearing   . . . Jesus' friend
Lazarus was ill, Jesus . . .   and sick.

Mary, Martha and   . . . would not end
Lazarus lived . . .   in death.

Jesus says that Lazarus'   . . . the people in Judea
sickness . . .   tried to stone Jesus.

When Jesus announces   . . . stayed where he
Lazarus has fallen asleep . . .   was for two more days.

For timing, it's important to know that this story begins about a week before Jesus is crucified. Jesus has been in Jerusalem for the Feast of Dedication, or Hanukkah. However, when the people threaten to stone Him for blasphemy, Jesus escapes (John 10:39) and travels to the region of Batanea, which is located northeast of Jerusalem and around one hundred miles away.[2]

While in Batanea, Jesus receives a report from Mary and Martha that their brother and his dear friend, Lazarus, is ill. The siblings aren't just casual acquaintances of Jesus. In fact, these are some of Jesus' really good friends. But Jesus doesn't spring into action. I don't know about you, but when I get a text message that a dear friend is in a life-or-death situation, I'll hurry to my car and go see about him or her.

Jesus stays put. In fact, this Gospel's author, John, makes note of it: "So although Jesus loved Martha, Mary, and Lazarus, he stayed where he was for the next two days" (John 11:5-6 NLT).

So what's going on here? Just before Jesus decided to stay put, he prophesied about Lazarus's illness, saying that it would not end in death. Not only that, but Jesus explains that Lazarus's illness actually has a higher purpose: "It happened for the glory of God so that the Son of God will receive glory from this" (John 11:4 NLT).

What do you think Jesus means when he says that Lazarus's illness will be for the glory of God?

In order to understand the greater lesson that Jesus is setting up for the disciples, Mary and Martha, and us, it is so important to understand what it means to see the glory of God on display. God's glory is found anywhere His greatness or authority is on display.[5] This means that we can keep our eyes on the lookout for God's glory or miss it depending on where we're looking for the perspective that we're clinging to in a particular situation or memory.

God's glory isn't elevated or diminished by our perspective or our particular situation. Every supernatural quality of God is true and perfect, no matter our situation. One of the hardest lessons that I've had to learn in my long waiting room journey is that God's greatness, goodness, beauty, or power isn't dependent on how He answers my prayers. It has been a hard lesson because, as Christians who live in a country with vast amounts of freedom and abundance compared to the rest of the world, we can fall into the trap of believing that positive answers to prayer are a sign of God's favor and blessing. But is that really true?

My friend Carine lives in Florida and feels this tension during hurricane season. One year a massive hurricane was forecast to slam into her community. I remember seeing the pleas for prayer on social media. At the last moment, the storm changed course and Hallelujah and Praise God filled my newsfeed. However, that same hurricane slammed into Mexico City, causing tremendous devastation. When we assign God's goodness to positive answers to prayers, we misrepresent the true nature of God to the world around us.

Why is the outcome of our prayers a flawed and dangerous way to interpret evidence of God's glory in our lives?

Hebrews 11 has been one of my favorite chapters of the Bible for many years. Not only does the writer begin by casting a vision of what faith looks like, but also many of my personal heroes are named. Yet toward the end of the chapter the names of biblical heroes who lived by great faith fade into the nameless multitudes who believed and trusted God yet had a different outcome.

Look up Hebrews 11:36-40. How did the lives of some of God's faithful end?

Recognizing our misinterpretation of God's glory is vital when we're facing a waiting room journey that may end with a no. It's so easy to shout "Glory to God" when a life is saved from death or a prodigal returns home. But why are we silent or reluctant to proclaim "Glory to God" in hard times? Is God's greatness worthy of proclamation only when you get what you want? How can you testify to God's glory to others, including those far from God, if the only time that you proclaim His glory is when He gives you what you want?

If we cannot say "Glory to God" in the good and the bad, then what kind of message are we sending about trusting God's sovereignty and character in all situations?

As Jesus talks to His disciples, He wants them to see beyond Lazarus's situation and begin looking for evidence of God's power and greatness, even through the coming grief and tears. This same lesson applies to us.

How has what you have read so far challenged or enlightened your understanding of God's glory in your life, especially as it pertains to your unanswered prayers?

Jesus replied, "There are twelve hours of daylight every day. During the day people can walk safely. They can see because they have the light of this world."

(John 11:9 NLT)

When Jesus spoke again to the people, he said, "I am the light of the world. Whoever follows me will never walk in darkness, but will have the light of life."

(John 8:12)

Jesus had been speaking of his death, but his disciples thought he meant natural sleep.

(John 11:13)

After two days, Jesus tells the disciples that it's time to see about Lazarus. Concerned questions come quickly. They're worried because Jesus wants to go back to the same place where his life was threatened only days before. Surely the people haven't forgotten Jesus' bold teaching in such a short period of time. They are concerned not only for Jesus but probably for themselves as well.

It's here that Jesus casts a wide vision extending beyond Lazarus's condition and their fears of violence.

Read John 11:9 and John 8:12 in the margin. As you consider both of these verses, what is Jesus saying about Himself and His mission in the world?

Now read John 11:13 in the margin. It seems that the disciples have misunderstood Jesus' words. What has happened to Lazarus?

We read that Lazarus has died. Furthermore, Jesus knows that Lazarus has died. My first thought is, "But Jesus could have done something about this!" That's something that I've struggled with often as a Christian, knowing that an all-powerful God can do something but being baffled when He doesn't. My heart goes out to Mary and Martha because they must have been at home watching their brother get weaker.

If social media had been available at that time, they would have posted urgent prayer requests. Not only that, but they would have expected Jesus to show up because he was their friend. He was in Batanea when he learned of Lazarus's illness and could have come immediately to heal His friend. It wasn't as if they'd expected preferential treatment. They knew Jesus healed many. So, if Jesus supernaturally helped and healed people that He didn't know, then why didn't He show up to heal Lazarus, someone that He did know?

When God doesn't provide your desired answer to prayer in time for rescue, relief, or survival, how does that affect the way that you see or trust God?

In his book Shattered Dreams, Christian psychologist Larry Crabb describes our problem with God. He talks about our struggle to understand why God doesn't step in to fix the painful things in our lives. He writes, "How do we trust a sometimes disappointing, seemingly fickle God who fails to do for us what good friends, if they could, would do?"[6]

In my life, I've struggled with why God continues to allow the addiction crisis in my family to divide us instead of reunite us. Maybe you're still wrestling with health issues, dysfunctional relationships, a dead-end job, or one Mr. Wrong after another. You're not alone if you've watched the clock run out and wondered why God never showed up. It's so important to your faith for you not to run from these hard questions. Give yourself permission to grapple with God.

In the Old Testament, there is a man named Jacob, whose name means deceiver. For much of his life, Jacob tricks people, but he can't trick God. Jacob wrestles hand-to-hand with God all night long in Genesis 32; you must wrestle with God as well if you want to be blessed

by God. I love that he fights with God all night long, and in Genesis 32:26 (CEB) he says: "I won't let you go until you bless me." My friend, that is the desire that I hope flourishes in your heart—that you won't let go of God until you've wrestled out the things that you struggle with or don't understand about your waiting room journey. In fact, one of the best blessings of any delayed prayer is when you have it out with God over the things that you don't understand.

Are you wrestling with God right now? Write down some of the things that you still don't understand or hate that you are going through:

I can see Martha sitting beside Lazarus as he takes his final breaths. Does she wrestle with frustration wondering, Why isn't Jesus here? Doesn't He know that time is running out?

Read John 11:17-19. How long has Lazarus been in his grave?

By the time that Jesus shows up in Bethany, Lazarus has been in his grave for four days. At this point, Martha has likely given up hope that Jesus can do anything to help her brother. Jesus has brought others back from the dead, such as Jairus's daughter (see Mark 5), but everyone Jesus has raised had not been buried.

It's important to note that Lazarus has been dead for four days. According to ancient beliefs in Jewish teaching, death was considered reversible within the first three days. One source explains, "For three days [after death] the soul hovers over the body, intending to re-enter it, but as soon as it sees its appearance change, it departs."[7] At that time it was believed that a person's face was recognizable for the first three days after death. Once the soul no longer recognized the face, it would depart.[8] So, based on ancient beliefs, I wonder if Lazarus's sisters held on to hope that maybe Jesus could show up within the first three days and still bring their brother back to life.

By the time that Jesus arrives, however, all lingering hope is gone. Martha and Mary aren't alone in their mourning. There's a crowd of people there to grieve with them. Since the Feast of Dedication has been going on in Jerusalem, many Jews would be in the city. Since Jerusalem was only a few miles away from the home of Lazarus, Martha, and Mary, many of those Jews have come to comfort Mary and Martha after hearing that Lazarus died. In the Jewish tradition, one of the important aspects of community is to show up and surround those who grieve—similar to the instructions that the apostle Paul teaches in Romans 12:15:

Rejoice with those who rejoice; mourn with those who mourn.

In my life, this verse reminds me to not forget that others are going through the ups and downs of life as well. Right after I wrote the Joshua Bible study, my dad died only eight days after being diagnosed with cancer. Between our ongoing family crisis and the grief of losing my dad, I had to fight hard against the waves of self-pity and the temptation of isolation. As I mindlessly scrolled through social media, I felt God's prompting to pray for people who were posting about having a hard time. I also posted quick notes celebrating birthdays, anniversaries, and family moments. It wasn't easy, but being a part of others' highs and lows actually helped me stay off the bitter road in my own journey.

Tomorrow we'll see what happens when Martha comes out to meet Jesus and consider some of the lessons we learn about how Martha experiences blessing even though Jesus doesn't come until after Lazarus is gone.

Memory Verse Reflection

As you finish today's study, take some time to reflect on this week's memory verse from Revelation 21:4. This verse makes me so excited because life can be pretty tough at times!

Fill in the missing blanks:

"He will wipe every _____ from their eyes. There will be no
more _____ or mourning or _____ or pain,
for the old order of things has passed away."

(*Revelation 21:4*)

Just as Mary and Martha watched their brother die, we've all faced the death of someone we love or the death of some part of our life that we deeply care about.

But God promises that one day, when He makes His home with us, we will have no more need for tears. That will mark the end of everything that we hate most on earth: death, mourning, crying, and pain.

What does Revelation 21:4 mean to you personally?

Prayer

God, I long for the day when You make all things right. I can't wait for the day when there is no more suffering, pain, or waiting rooms. Until then, I will bring my hard questions and heartache to You.

Today, God, I am afraid that it might be too late for _____

_____.

I need to trust that even if You don't answer my prayer according to my desire or timeline, that doesn't mean that You don't love me or that Your best isn't waiting for me; in Jesus' name. Amen.

Today's Takeaway

It's okay for me to wrestle with God over my tough questions.

Day 2: Jesus Understands How You Feel

Gratitude Moment

Today I am grateful to God for _____

_____

_____

_____.

WAITING ROOM PRINCIPLE

When you let go of your dead dreams, God plants new ones in the fertile soil of faith and trust.

This week our waiting room problem is how to find hope when time seems to run out and our waiting room journey ends with a no. This is the question that Martha faces as her brother dies and Jesus shows up after Lazarus is in the grave.

Jesus purposefully doesn't show up until after Lazarus's death, even though He knows that Martha and Mary will experience tremendous grief. As much as we hate to grieve, it is an important part of life that we all experience. We not only mourn the loss of loved ones but also the loss of our hopes and dreams. Grief plays an important role in helping us accept that pain and disconnection are part of our fallen world. The only way toward health and healing is to embrace grief, fully feel it, and then learn the practice of releasing it back to God.

One day each spring I pack a blanket, my Bible, a notebook, and a packet of tissues. Then I drive down to a beautiful river a few miles from my house. First, I lay out my blanket on a patch of grass overlooking the water. Then I open up my notebook and begin listing all my unanswered prayers, unmet expectations, and unfilled dreams of the past year. These are the things that have died in my life. On that day, I need to go through the process of letting go of lost time, lost opportunities, or lost options. Holding on to what has died isn't healthy or helpful. Letting go is painful but important. I call this exercise my annual funeral.

Since funerals usually mean a lot of tears, I find a secluded space so as not to draw too much attention to myself. For whatever reason, this exercise works best for me when I'm outdoors under the vast sky that reminds me of God's glory (Psalm 19:1). My goal is to empty myself of dreams and desires that have died or never will be. So, I'm often writing with one hand and wiping my tears with a tissue in the other. The sentences in my notebook begin with phrases such as, "I really hoped," "I wished," "I truly thought," or "I prayed so hard that..." Here are some of my funeral notebook entries:

- I wished that I had more time with my dad...
- God, I really prayed hard for You to remove the addiction from our home...
- God, I hoped so much for a chance to speak at that event...

Once I empty myself of disappointments and dead dreams, I grab my Bible and read pre-marked verses on hope such as Jeremiah 29:11 and Isaiah 61:13. These verses do not make me feel better immediately, but these words are a reminder of God's glory, greatness, and power beyond my circumstances.

> "I know the plans I have for you," declares the LORD, "plans to prosper you and not to harm you, plans to give you hope and a future."
>
> (Jeremiah 29:11)

> ¹The Spirit of the Sovereign LORD is on me,
>   because the LORD has anointed me
>   to proclaim good news to the poor.
> He has sent me to bind up the brokenhearted,
>   to proclaim freedom for the captives
>   and release from darkness for the prisoners, . . .

Extra Insight

"Occasionally weep deeply over the life that you hoped would be. Grieve the losses. Feel the pain. Then wash your face, trust God, and embrace the life that he's given you."
–John Piper[9]

Funeral Prayer

I dreamed that (name dream), but that dream isn't going to come true. I really wanted it, God! And it hurts. But I need to let that dream die. I need to mourn it and move it out of my heart so that You can fill the space with a new thing for me.

Extra Insight

God's "no" is not a rejection. It's a redirection.

– Anonymous

²*to comfort all who mourn,*
³*and provide for those who grieve in Zion—*
to bestow on them a crown of beauty
instead of ashes,
the oil of joy
instead of mourning,
and a garment of praise
instead of a spirit of despair.
They will be called oaks of righteousness,
a planting of the Lord
for the display of his splendor.

(Isaiah 61:1-3)

Finally, I pray and surrender what will not be. It's an ugly cry prayer with words that are often unintelligible, but I trust God's Holy Spirit to speak when I can't say the words. My funeral prayer is in the margin. I've learned that carrying around dead or dying dreams eventually deadens our hearts. A dead heart can't receive a beautiful blessing.

What I've learned over the past decade of having an annual funeral is that when I let go of my dead dreams, God plants new ones in the fertile soil of faith that has formed as I fought in prayer for those dying dreams or desires.

Do you need to have a funeral? Here are three indicators in my life that I need to let go of something:

1. The opportunity or experience is no longer possible, even if I want it to be.
2. The person or people involved are not willingly cooperating.
3. I sense that God is calling me to let it go.

As painful as it is to face what you've lost, this process allows you to make space for God to move in and fill that space with more of Him, if you are willing.

You have permission to have a funeral right now, if necessary. Or you might choose to have one later today or this week.

Now it's time to find out what happens when Jesus arrives. This is a highly emotional encounter on many levels. In the face of a waiting room journey that ends differently than desired, you'll witness a side of Jesus' humanity that will remind you that God sees all of your tears and cries with you. Then you'll witness the power of God at work, celebrate the display of His glory in Mary's situation, and discover how you can experience the blessing of God's glory in your life, too.

Read John 11:20-27. Answer the following questions:

Martha goes out to meet Jesus, but where does her sister, Mary, stay?

What does Martha say to Jesus in verse 21?

How does Jesus respond to Martha?

Jesus has arrived at Martha and Mary's home, but it's several days after their brother, Lazarus, has died. It's not hard to imagine grieving sisters and the friends who have traveled from Jerusalem to comfort them.

The scene of Martha going out to meet Jesus has been interpreted many ways. For those who picture the no-nonsense Martha from her actions and words in Luke 10:40, her greeting to Jesus in John 11:21 may sound like a scolding. If we read her words at face value, Martha sounds like a woman who is disappointed but who unconditionally loves Jesus and trusts His divine authority in her life.

Do you think that Martha is scolding Jesus or simply stating the facts? Why?

I choose to see Martha's faith in her words. In essence, Martha is saying, "Jesus, I'm glad that You're here, but can You still help?" She knows that Jesus is the Messiah, so even though her brother has died and has been in the grave beyond the three-day mark, Martha still has hope. In John 11:22 (CEB), Martha says, "Even now I know that whatever you ask God, God will give you."

We'll come back to Jesus' response to Martha in a moment. Now let's catch up with Mary.

Read John 11:28-32, and answer the following questions: When Martha goes to Mary to tell her that Jesus has arrived, who accompanies Mary and Martha back to see Him?

What does Mary say to Jesus in verse 32?

If you notice, as soon as Martha and Mary approach Jesus, they both make the same declaration: "Lord, if you had been here, my brother wouldn't have died" (verses 21, 32 CEB) As much as those words may declare faith in Jesus' power and ability to do miracles, do they also carry an underlying expectation that Jesus should have come to heal Lazarus?

Though the women say the same thing, Jesus responds differently.

Read John 11:23-26, and summarize Jesus' response to Martha below:

Now read John 11:33-35. How does Jesus respond to Mary's statement?

Extra Insight

"Jesus boldly challenged Martha to trust that He was the source of eternal life. Jesus presented Himself as the champion over death. While humanity in general fears death, the Christian can only fear dying. The believer will never die, but simply make an instant transition from an old life to a new life."[10]

Two different women receive two different responses. Jesus speaks to Martha and Mary as individuals who are seen, known, and loved individually by God. Pastor Tim Keller observes that Martha receives the ministry of truth while Mary receives the ministry of tears.[11] While Martha needs Jesus to affirm the eternal nature of His divine purpose, Mary needs to experience Jesus' presence and compassion to know that He understands her pain. Jesus ministers to each woman exactly where she is spiritually. Jesus doesn't condemn Martha's forthrightness, nor does he criticize Mary's tears.

There's much that we can learn from Jesus' approach, especially when we're mourning a prayer that wasn't answered as hoped. Ecclesiastes 3:1 teaches us that there is a time and place for everything under heaven. There is a time and place to apply the ministry of truth. As Jesus converses with Martha, he lifts her focus from her present situation to His eternal perspective. As Jesus affirms His identity as the resurrection and the life, He wants Martha to remember that in Him, life never ends. Jesus wants to get Martha unstuck in her current situation.

It's the truth of Jesus that will set your heart and mind free from the bondage of thinking only about what is in front you. Therefore, you need to run after the ministry of truth when your mind is stuck on the past or you can't see beyond your present circumstance. You also may need to offer the ministry of truth when a friend asks for advice and you are able to offer gentle correction (Galatians 6:1-2).

Whom do you relate to more, Martha or Mary?

Is there a place in your waiting room situation where you need to apply the ministry of truth to your life or someone else's?

The ministry of tears or presence is equally important—whether for yourself or someone else. This requires humility because when people are in pain, we think that it's best to talk ourselves out of our pain or endeavor to pull someone else out of their pain. We don't realize that a heart in pain is more willing to cry out for God. So, the ministry of presence is often silence and a hug. All "you should's" must be canceled and all blackboard-screeching clichés avoided. Scrolling through Twitter one day, Rick Warren's post caught my eye and blessed my heart: "When people are in deep pain they don't need explanations, advice, encouragement, or even Scripture. They just need you to show up and shut up. Just be WITH them. It's the healing ministry of presence."[12]

How can you know when to apply the ministry of truth versus the ministry of tears? Here's a catchy little ditty that I made up to help you remember:

> When someone is crying,
> tissues, listening ears, and chocolate you should be
> supplying.

> When someone is stuck, stubborn, or disgusted,
> sharing the freeing power of Jesus' truth must be trusted.

Is there a place in your waiting room situation where you need to apply the ministry of tears or presence to your life or someone else's?

As Jesus offers the ministry of presence to Mary, He also notices the pain and anguish of the crowd surrounding her, like a group of people surrounding you at your loved one's funeral. The group feels Martha's and Mary's pain. We all know the breathtaking crush of death and suffocating weight of grief. Jesus feels their pain. He is deeply moved—not as a bystander but as God Himself standing in their midst. The Greek word that describes Jesus' emotional reaction to their pain is *embrimaomai*, or a "snorting anger," such as how an animal snorts.[13] More than just sadness over His friend's death, we see Jesus' righteous anger over human suffering as a consequence of sin. Jesus shows His emotions, and John describes it in the shortest verse in the Bible.

Look up John 11:35 and write the verse below:

Jesus cried. If Jesus cried, you can, too! God gave us tears because sometimes there are no words for what we feel. It's okay to cry!

In the following verses, John shares some whispers from the crowd. There were those who witnessed Jesus' tears and were touched by Jesus' love for Lazarus. Others questioned why, if Jesus could perform miracles, He didn't perform one here.

Imagine you are in the crowd that day. What is going through your mind as you see Jesus crying in front of Lazarus's tomb?

One of the reasons Jesus came to earth is to show us what God is really like. Lazarus's death allows us to see the visible anger and anguish that God feels on our behalf. More than just tears for a friend, Jesus' tears are shed for the anguish of humanity, broken and condemned by sin. And only a week later Jesus' blood will be shed to snatch humanity from condemnation and usher in restoration and redemption.

But before Jesus begins His final journey toward His crucifixion and death, He's going to show Martha, Mary, and the crowd a symbol of His power.

Prayer

God, help me see if there are any unanswered prayers or dead dreams that I'm still carrying in my heart. I do not want those painful disappointments to occupy my soul. Instead, God, I want to surrender them and make room for You to do something new in my life. Like Martha, I believe that there is everlasting life in You; and like Mary, I may need to shed a few tears over what is lost. Either way, I am grateful for Your loving compassion and presence no matter what end of the spectrum I'm at today. Thank You for seeing me, knowing me, and loving me as I am. Amen.

Today's Takeaway

Jesus feels your pain when your dream dies.

Day 3: The Impossible Can Happen at Any Time

Today is the final day of our Bible study, even though you still have one more optional self-study and devotional. I hope that as you've learned about Hannah, Ruth, the unnamed bleeding woman, and Martha, your own waiting room journey has been transformed from panic to peace, from anguish to anticipation, or from fighting to faith and endurance. Even if you're still feeling a little impatient, I trust that God is still working! I'm learning that patience is a life-long process, not a one-time prize. Rather than expecting that I will always be patient, I choose to celebrate that I have God-given tools to experience patience anytime that I am willing to use those tools.

As I've written this study from my long-time waiting room, I am grateful for the experiences that have allowed me to relate to your painful waiting spaces. Or if you're not in a waiting room journey, I hope that this study is equipping you for the future.

Do you recall Cherise's story at the beginning of this week? It is actually my own personal story. Writing this Bible study on unanswered prayer has exposed the real and raw edges of my heart. While I am grateful to be a Bible study teacher and writer, what I am first is a child of God who must walk out her own faith journey during a hard season. There are no shortcuts for any of us, including me! I've had to fight to find my blessings when God's answer to my decade-long prayer was no. I still believe that God can do the impossible, but I've also found tremendous

Gratitude Moment

Today I am grateful to God for _____

_____

_____

_____

_____

blessings of greater faith even as God has allowed the good life that I deeply loved to end.

As you finish up Martha and Jesus' story today, you will join them at Lazarus's tomb where a miracle is about to happen. However, don't limit the story to the miracle; rather, see the purpose behind the miracle. That's where the blessing lies for you. You can count on this: If God lets your good dream die, He has a better blessing waiting for you.

It's okay if you're having a hard time accepting that God could allow good dreams or desires to die in your life. Remember Laura Story's words: "Sometimes God uses things he hates . . . to accomplish the things he loves."[14] God hates death, adultery, barrenness/infertility, divorce, abuse, addiction, idolatry, and so much more. Yet God also allows those things to demolish the gates of our white-picket-fence expectations because He doesn't want our goal in life to be comfort. He wants our goal in life to be worshiping Him alone. And there are times, even as we don't understand why, that God allows the consequences of our broken world to break our hearts in ways that steal the breath from our lungs and bring us to our knees.

Even so, God always has a better blessing when that good thing we love or have been praying for is lost to us forever.

Extra Insight

"God is always working to make His children aware of a dream that remains alive beneath the rubble of every shattered dream, a new dream that when realized will release a new song, sung with tears, till God wipes them away and we sing with nothing but joy in our hearts."

–Larry Crabb[15]

Read John 11:38-40, and answer the following questions:

What does Jesus order?

What is Martha's objection to Jesus' command?

As one with a heart for hospitality, Martha doesn't want everyone's senses to suffer the assault of Lazarus's decomposing body. However, as she focuses on the practical aspects of Jesus' command, she may have forgotten who she is speaking to.

How does Jesus respond to Martha's concerns in verse 40?

In another moment when Jesus ministers truth to Martha, He reminds her that faith in Him makes the impossible, possible. So the stone is removed, and Jesus looks up and prays to God in a manner similar to that of the prophet Elijah in 1 Kings 18:36-37, when he was at Mount Carmel in a standoff against Baal's prophets.

Read John 11:43-44.

What does Jesus call out?

What happens next? How does Lazarus come out of the tomb?

Extra Insight

"In this short prayer we see no prayer for healing of the man who had lain dead for four days. Just a simple thank-you in advance. This could be interpreted either as presumptuous or faith-filled."[16]

Jesus calls Lazarus out of his tomb. At other times Jesus would be physically near the person, but in this case, he calls Lazarus back to life. Talk about an attention grabber!

Consider what it would have been like to be a friend who showed up to offer your condolences to Martha and Mary. Then you see Jesus show up, and the crowd whispers their opinions about Him. Next, you're in front of Lazarus's tomb, no doubt wondering if you should drift to the back of the crowd to avoid some of the smell. You see Jesus standing in front of the tomb praying to God. Then Jesus raises His voice and says, "Lazarus, come out!" (verse 43).

I'm not exactly sure what I would do in that moment, but panic comes to mind. What if Lazarus comes out? What if he doesn't?

Lazarus does come out. He is alive. There's no information on what kind of condition he's in; but since he's no longer dead and has walked out of the tomb on his own, that says a lot!

The story abruptly shifts after that point to the reaction of the crowd. Many in the crowd have come to believe that Jesus is the Messiah. Others run to the religious leaders to tell them about Lazarus coming back from the dead. The events that follow set into motion a plan to kill Jesus, which will unfold over the coming Passover week.

If you're wondering what happens to Lazarus, Mary, and Martha, keep reading John 12. A couple of days later, a dinner is given in Jesus' honor. Lazarus is listed as one of the people with Jesus, as well as Martha who is serving the meal. At this dinner, Mary pours an exquisite, expensive perfume on Jesus' feet and wipes His feet with her hair. Sadly, the newly revived Lazarus becomes the target of the religious leaders who want to kill him because the story of his resurrection has influenced many people

Verses About God's Better Blessing for You

You will show me the way of life,
granting me the joy of your presence and the pleasures of living with you forever.
(Psalm 16:11 NLT)

"You must love the LORD your God with all your heart, all your soul, all your mind, and all your strength."
(Mark 12:30 NLT)

I pray that God, the source of hope, will fill you completely with joy and peace because you trust in him. Then you will overflow with confident hope through the power of the Holy Spirit.
(Romans 15:13 NLT)

Take delight in the LORD,
and he will give you your heart's desires.
(Psalm 37:4 NLT)

to follow Jesus. In many ways Lazarus's resurrection has propelled the events of Jesus' arrest forward.

While Lazarus's illness does not end in final death, the truth is that, eventually, Lazarus will die again. So, the point of this story, or even of Martha's suffering, isn't that Jesus brings her brother back to life; it's that Lazarus's illness, death, and revival set up the scene for Jesus to give His life for the redemption of our sins.

So, while Lazarus did die, Jesus used that time of suffering and loss to draw Martha's attention to the greater and better blessing that is life eternal in Christ. This principle is what inspires the waiting room principle: If God lets your good dream die, He has a better blessing waiting for you. And it comes down to this question: Do you understand God's ultimate blessing for you? If you think that God's better blessing for your life is comfort, a new car every few years, healthy children, a long marriage, or financial stability, then the end of any of those things will uproot any faith you have in His glory. While God does bless you with those good things, and it's good to celebrate them, the ongoing presence of those things in your life cannot compare to finding your life in God Himself.

What is God's better blessing for you?

In my waiting room journey, I've been surprised by some of the blessings that I've experienced even as years passed with my prayers seeming to get stuck and then end with a painful no. Those blessings quietly stacked up in my life over the days, months, and years of inching toward Jesus with my heart, mind, and soul.

In fact, it wasn't until a recent New Year's Eve that I sat down and listed some of those blessings. Earlier that day I'd been struggling with the suffering and pain I'd experienced as a consequence of my waiting room no. As I reflected on the year, I grabbed my notebook and wrote down the faith lessons that I've learned, the strengths that I've gained, and the courage that I displayed. I was astonished that I filled an entire sheet of paper and had to start writing in the margins.

Here are some of the lessons that have become blessings that have drawn me to God, improved how I love others, and increased the peace and joy in my life:

- When I am patient, I don't have to push for solutions because God drops provision in place.
- Forgiveness is a path that I must walk over and over again.
- I am not responsible for fixing other people's problems, only for having faith that God will help me with mine.
- Be a blessing instead of looking for one.
- Stay focused on God's future for me, not what I see in front of me.
- I can do big things even in hard times.

Now, it's your turn.

Write down the strengths that you've gained, the faith that you've found, or the courage that you've displayed during your waiting journey.

Can you describe how those lessons have blessed your life? Do you sense an increasing connection to God, peace, joy, or hope?

If a waiting room journey in your life has ended or seems to be ending with a no, know that there is life beyond that no. It's here that faith is needed. Instead of fixing our eyes on what we want, we must trust God and focus on His direction for our next steps beyond the no. When we trust God, our better blessing is found beyond the no.

WAITING ROOM APPLICATION

Trust that your story has evidence of God's glory. Reflect on some of the blessings that you've experienced during your season of waiting.

Today's Takeaway

You may not always get the outcome that you want, but God is always willing to give the better blessings that you need.

Prayer

God, trusting You when the outcome is different than I'd hoped is really hard. Yet I want to experience the better blessing that You have for my life. Enable me to see where You've helped me to mature and grow during my waiting seasons. Give me opportunities to share the better blessings that You've given me to help others; in Jesus' name. Amen.

Bible Story Wrap-Up

As you studied Martha this week, I hope that you noticed how she never gave up on having faith, even when her prayer went unanswered. Even more than that, I love that Jesus responded to Mary and Martha according to what their deepest need was in their time of grief. He will do the same for you, especially if you've experienced an outcome opposite of what you had hoped. As our memory verse reminds us this week, there will come a day when God will make all things right. There will come a day when there will be no more tears, unfulfilled expectations, or disappointments. Until that day comes, my friend, I pray that you follow in Martha's footsteps and keep walking by faith and trusting in Christ's power.

Now that we have come to the end of Martha's story, take a moment to consider what you have learned and how God is calling you to respond.

What are one or two things that you've learned from Martha's life this week?

How is God prompting you to think or live differently as a result of what you've heard or learned this week?

Day 4: Self-Study (*Optional*)

Today you have the opportunity to participate in an optional self-study with a Bible verse or passage of your choosing. The Verse Bank on page 146 features Scriptures that fit thematically with Martha. Select one of the Scriptures listed and follow these prompts.

Read

Write below the verse or passage you selected:

Reflect

Now open your Bible and read a few verses that precede and follow your chosen Scripture in order to gather a bigger picture of what is going on. Use study helps as needed or desired to answer questions such as these: Who is speaking? Who is the audience? When or where were these words written? What is the overarching message? Are there any words that you need to look up for better understanding? (Check out Bible search websites such as BibleGateway.com and others for commentaries, Bible dictionaries, and other tools.) Write your responses below.

Respond

Ask yourself the question: How does God want me to think or live differently as a result of what I've read? Consider how you can apply this passage to your life.

Release

Write a prayer to God expressing that you are willing to apply what you've learned to your life.

Day 5: Devotional and Prayer Journaling
(Optional)

¹The Spirit of the Sovereign Lord is on me,
    because the Lord has anointed me
    to proclaim good news to the poor.
He has sent me to bind up the brokenhearted,
    to proclaim freedom for the captives
    and release from darkness for the prisoners, . . .

²to comfort all who mourn,
*   ³and provide for those who grieve in Zion—*
to bestow on them a crown of beauty
*   instead of ashes,*
the oil of joy
*   instead of mourning*
and a garment of praise
*   instead of a spirit of despair.*
They will be called oaks of righteousness,
*   a planting of the Lord*
*   for the display of his splendor.*

(Isaiah 61:1-3)

Gratitude Moment

Today I am grateful to God for _____

_____

_____

_____

_____.

On September 10, 2001, singer Tammy Trent sat on the edge of a beautiful lagoon in Jamaica as her husband, Trent Linderink, went for a free dive underwater. He was only supposed to be gone for fifteen minutes. She never saw Trent alive again.

Tammy and Trent began dating when they were teens and married after seven years. After Tammy signed her record contract, Trent left his family business to join Tammy on the road. Just before that mission trip to Jamaica, Tammy and Trent began talking about the next season of their lives. After eleven years of marriage, they were ready to finally start a family.

On the same day as the September 11 attacks in America, divers recovered Trent's body in Jamaica. When Tammy got the news, she was devastated and numb. There were so many questions. One of the many questions she asked was, "God, how could you see this being good for my life?"[17]

Until the day that God makes all things new and wipes all of the tears from our eyes, our broken world will break our hearts. But long ago the prophet Isaiah prophesied a message from Jesus to God's people about why He had to come and what He came to do.

There are so many rich descriptions of restoration in this passage, but I love the phrase "a crown of beauty instead of ashes." In ancient times, ashes were a symbol of grief. In the face of grief, beauty feels impossible. But in Christ, beauty in the midst of great sadness and pain is not only possible but promised.

I've seen that crown of beauty atop many of the heads of courageous friends, such as Kaila and Jamey, who lost two newborn sons, Samuel and Gabriel, six years apart. Both boys had the same genetic disorder and only lived a short time after birth. Now Kaila writes for an international

magazine publication sharing hope and faith with other mothers who have suffered infant loss.

For the past decade as our family has struggled through an addiction crisis, I've been overwhelmed how God has made beauty from ashes—whether it was the blessing that came from the obedience to forgive or the obedience to endure. At other times, I've seen God use my story to point others to Jesus.

I don't know where you need Jesus to heal the space that won't be filled with what you want. I'm not sure what you're mourning. But I do know that God can bring beauty from it if you let Him. The choice is yours. And if you're still holding on and waiting for God to answer your prayer, keep holding on, my friend. Don't give up until you sense God is calling you to let go.

Recently, I heard Tammy on a podcast interview where she was asked about the future. She gave an answer that I hope might cast a vision for you, especially if you want to find God's best blessing for your future. Here's what she said:

> ...I'm gonna stand on faith that what seems impossible will become possible if it lines up with Your will for my life. Yes, I have lots of dreams and I have lots of things that I want to do and goals, but Father, if it doesn't line up with your will for my life, then get rid of it, take away the desire.... If it's God's way, He will always bring you to the other side of it where you will be able to look back and say, "It was worth it all."[18]

Martha

Embracing the Better Blessing

God's better blessing is and always will be with Him.

Welcome/Prayer/Icebreaker (5-10 minutes)

Welcome to Session 4 of *I'm Waiting, God*. This week we've considered how we can find hope when our waiting room journey ends with a no. Today we're exploring what Martha has to teach us about experiencing God's better blessing. Take a moment to open with prayer, and then go around the circle and share a time when you experienced an unexpected blessing.

Video (about 20 minutes)

Play the Group Centering video for Week 4 (optional), taking a couple of minutes to focus your hearts and minds on God and God's Word. Then play the video segment for Week 4, filling in the blanks as you watch and making notes about anything that resonates with you or that you want to be sure to remember.

—Video Notes—

Scripture: John 11:4, Romans 8:28, John 11:21, John 11:35, John 11:33, Romans 6:23, Matthew 6:20, Matthew 27:46, Revelation 21:4

When I walk by faith, my waiting story will have evidence of _____ _____.

When God says no, I must let go so God can reposition me for His _____ _____.

For every "no" we face, we have the hope of a _____ _____.

Other Insights:

Group Discussion (20-25 minutes for a 60-minute session; 30-35 minutes for a 90-minute session)

Video Discussion

- Have you ever been angry with God when His answer to your prayer was no? Share briefly about that time and how you processed your anger.
- How does letting go of our anger and bitterness position us for God's better blessing?
- How does believing that our story is for God's glory help us trust Him in times of waiting?

Workbook Discussion

- What happens in John 11? Piece together the story in your own words.
- What does Jesus say in 11:6? Why would he stay put when his good friends were suffering?
- Read John 11:4. What do you think Jesus means when he says that Lazarus's illness will be for the glory of God? (page 112)
- Why is the outcome of our prayers a flawed and dangerous way to interpret the evidences of God's glory in our lives? (page 113)
- *"If Jesus supernaturally helped and healed people that He didn't know, then why didn't He show up to heal Lazarus, someone that He did know?"* When God doesn't provide your desired answer to prayer in time for rescue, relief, or survival, how does that affect the way that you see or trust God? (page 115)
- *"As much as we hate to grieve, it is an important part of life that we all experience. We not only mourn the loss of loved ones but also the loss of our hopes and dreams. Grief plays an important role in helping us accept that pain and disconnection are part of our fallen world. The only way toward health and healing is to embrace grief, fully feel it, and then learn the practice of releasing it back to God."* (pages 118–119) What is your experience with grief? Why is grief the only way toward healing?
- Read aloud Revelation 21:4. What does this verse mean to you personally? (page 118)

- Read John 11:20-27. What does Martha say to Jesus? How does Jesus respond to Martha? (page 121) What tone do you hear in their exchange? Do you think that Martha is scolding Jesus or simply stating the facts? Why? (page 121) What tone do you tend to take with Jesus in your distress and despair?
- *"Jesus ministers to each woman exactly where she is spiritually. Jesus doesn't condemn Martha's forthrightness, nor does he criticize Mary's tears."* (page 122) Whom do you relate to more, Martha or Mary? Why? (page 123)
- Read John 11:25. What does it mean to you that Jesus cried?
- *"While Lazarus did die, Jesus used that time of suffering and loss to draw Martha's attention to the greater and better blessing that is life eternal in Christ."* (page 128) What is God's better blessing for you? When has God let your good dream die in order to bring a better blessing into your life?

Learning to Wait (10-15 minutes – 90-minute session only)

Divide into groups of two or three and discuss the following (see page 130):

- What are one or two things you've learned from Martha's life this week?
- How is God prompting you to think or live differently as a result of what you've heard or learned?

Closing Prayer (5 minutes)

Close the session by sharing personal prayer requests and praying together. If you like, invite the women to surround those who have shared requests and pray for them aloud. In addition to praying aloud for one another, close by asking God to help you hold on to the hope of a better future and look for evidence of His glory in the midst of your waiting stories.

Self-Study
Verse Bank

"Be still, and know that I am God;

> I will be exalted among the nations,
> I will be exalted in the earth."
>
> > (Psalm 46:10)

"I know the plans I have for you," declares the LORD, "plans to prosper you and not to harm you, plans to give you hope and a future."

> (Jeremiah 29:11)

As for me, I watch in hope for the LORD,
> I wait for God my Savior;
> my God will hear me.
>
> > (Micah 7:7)

Blessed are you who hunger now,
> for you will be satisfied.
Blessed are you who weep now,
> for you will laugh.
>
> > (Luke 6:21)

If we hope for what we do not yet have, we wait for it patiently.
> > (Romans 8:25)

²⁵The LORD is good to those whose hope is in him,
   to the one who seeks him;
²⁶it is good to wait quietly
   for the salvation of the LORD.

(Lamentations 3:25-26)

"I will repay you for the years the locusts have eaten—
   the great locust and the young locust,
   the other locusts and the locust swarm—
my great army that I sent among you."

(Joel 2:25)

Let us not become weary in doing good, for at the proper time we will reap a harvest if we do not give up.

(Galatians 6:9)

Now to him who is able to do immeasurably more than all we ask or imagine, according to his power that is at work within us.

(Ephesians 3:20)

Wait for the LORD;
    be strong and take heart
    and wait for the LORD.
            (Psalm 27:14)

From the ends of the earth I call to you,
    I call as my heart grows faint;
    lead me to the rock that is higher than I.
                    (Psalm 61:2)

"Ah, Sovereign LORD, you have made the heavens and the earth by your great power and outstretched arm. Nothing is too hard for you."

                            (Jeremiah 32:17)

Put on the full armor of God, so that when the day of evil comes, you may be able to stand your ground, and after you have done everything, to stand.

                            (Ephesians 6:13)

Week 4: Martha

The revelation awaits an appointed time;
   it speaks of the end
   and will not prove false.
Though it linger, wait for it;
   it will certainly come
   and will not delay.

                         (Habakkuk 2:3)

I consider that our present sufferings are not worth comparing with the glory that will be revealed in us.

                         (Romans 8:18)

We fix our eyes not on what is seen, but on what is unseen, since what is seen is temporary, but what is unseen is eternal.

                         (2 Corinthians 4:18)

[12]Dear friends, do not be surprised at the fiery ordeal that has come on you to test you, as though something strange were happening to you. [13]But rejoice inasmuch as you participate in the sufferings of Christ, so that you may be overjoyed when his glory is revealed.

                         (1 Peter 4:12-13)

Leader Helps

Tips for Facilitating a Group

Important Information

Before the first session you will want to distribute copies of this study guide to the members of your group. Be sure to communicate that, if possible, they are to complete the first week in the study guide before your first group session.

As you gather each week with the members of your group, you will have the opportunity to watch a video, discuss and respond to what you're learning, and pray together. You will need access to a television and DVD player with working remotes. Use the Group Session Guide at the end of each week's lessons to facilitate the session (options are provided for both a 60-minute and a 90-minute format). In addition to these guides, the Group Session Guide Leader Notes (pages 151–154) provide additional helps including a Main Objective, Key Scripture reference, and Bible Story Overview for each session.

Creating a warm and inviting atmosphere will help to make the women feel welcome. Although optional, you might consider providing snacks for your first meeting and inviting group members to rotate in bringing refreshments each week.

As group leader, your role is to guide and encourage the women on the journey to discovering that their lives matter in God's great story. Pray that God would pour out His Spirit on your time together, that the Spirit would speak into each woman's life and circumstances, and that your group would grow in community together.

Preparing for the Sessions

- Be sure to communicate dates and times to participants in advance.
- Be sure that group members have their workbooks at least one week before your first session and instruct them to complete the first week of personal lessons in the study guide. If you have the phone numbers

or email addresses of your group members, send out a reminder and a welcome.

- Check out your meeting space before each group session. Make sure the room is ready. Do you have enough chairs? Do you have the equipment and supplies you need? (See the list of materials that follows.)
- Pray for your group and each group member by name. Ask God to work in the life of every woman in your group.
- Read and complete the week's readings in this study guide and review the group session guide. Select the discussion points and questions you want to make sure to cover and make some notes in the margins to share in your discussion time.

Leading the Sessions

- Personally welcome and greet each woman as she arrives. Take attendance if desired.
- In order to create a warm, welcoming environment as the women are gathering, consider lighting one or more candles, providing coffee or other refreshments, and/or playing worship music. (Bring an iPod, smartphone, or tablet and a portable speaker if desired.) Be sure to provide name tags if the women do not know one another or you have new participants in your group.
- Always start on time. Honor the time of those who are on time.
- At the start of each session, ask the women to turn off or silence their cell phones.
- Communicate the importance of completing the weekly lessons and participating in group discussion.
- Encourage everyone to participate fully, but don't put anyone on the spot. Invite the women to share as they are comfortable. Be prepared to offer a personal example or answer if no one else responds at first.
- Facilitate but don't dominate. Remember that if you talk most of the time, group members may tend to listen rather than to engage. Your task is to encourage conversation and keep the discussion moving.
- If someone monopolizes the conversation, kindly thank her for sharing and ask if anyone else has any insights.
- Try not to interrupt, judge, or minimize anyone's comments or input.

- Remember that you are not expected to be the expert or have all the answers. Acknowledge that all of you are on this journey together, with the Holy Spirit as your leader and guide. If issues or questions arise that you don't feel equipped to handle or answer, talk with the pastor or a staff member at your church.
- Don't rush to fill the silence. If no one speaks right away, it's okay to wait for someone to answer. After a moment, ask, "Would anyone be willing to share?" If no one responds, try asking the question again a different way—or offer a brief response and ask if anyone has anything to add.
- Encourage good discussion, but don't be timid about calling time on a particular question and moving ahead. Part of your responsibility is to keep the group on track. If you decide to spend extra time on a given question or activity, consider skipping or spending less time on another question or activity in order to stay on schedule.
- Do your best to end on time. If you are running over, give members the opportunity to leave if they need to. Then wrap up as quickly as you can.
- Thank the women for coming and let them know you're looking forward to seeing them next time.
- Be prepared for some women to want to hang out and talk at the end. If you need everyone to leave by a certain time, communicate this at the beginning of the group session. If you are meeting in a church during regularly scheduled activities, be aware of nursery closing times.

Materials Needed
- I'm Waiting, God workbook
- I'm Waiting, God DVD and a DVD player
- Stick-on name tags and markers (optional)
- iPod, smartphone, or tablet, and portable speaker (if desired for gathering music)

Group Session Guide Leader Notes

Use these notes for your own review and preparation. If desired, you can share the Main Objective, Key Scripture, and Bible Story Overview with the group at the beginning of the session to set the tone for the session, as well as prepare everyone for content discussion, especially those who might have been unable to complete their personal lessons during the week.

Session 1: Hannah: From Waiting to Worshiping

MAIN OBJECTIVE

To teach us how to turn our waiting into worshiping.

SCRIPTURE FOCUS

1 Samuel 1

BIBLE STORY OVERVIEW

This week we studied the story of Hannah in 1 Samuel. Hannah struggled with infertility for many years and pleaded with God to give her a son. She prayed so demonstratively in the house of the Lord once that Eli, the priest, thought she had been drinking. Her desperate prayer caused her to promise God that if He would give her a son, she would give that son right back to God. And some time later God responded to her many years of struggle, desperation, and praying by giving her a son, Samuel. She did give Samuel back to God, and he became a priest who was a key leader in the grand story of God.

Session 2: Ruth: God, Now What?

MAIN OBJECTIVE

To help us choose the better road rather than the bitter road.

SCRIPTURE FOCUS

Ruth 1–3

BIBLE STORY OVERVIEW

This week we read the Book of Ruth in which we find the story of Ruth, Naomi, and Orpah. Ruth and Orpah were married to Naomi's sons; and through a series of tragedies, the three women found themselves widowed and without resources. Ruth was committed to taking care of Naomi, and the two set out on a new life together, heading back to Naomi's hometown, Bethlehem. Orpah had gone back to her family. When they reached Bethlehem, Naomi told the women there to call her "Bitter" because God has made her bitter. But God would change that bitterness into blessing when Ruth met Boaz. Ruth set out to work the fields and provide for herself and for Naomi. When she was working, Boaz (Naomi's closest living relative) came on the scene. Boaz showed Ruth kindness and took care of her. Naomi made a bold plan for Ruth to ask Boaz to marry her so that they would be safe and secure. Boaz had to take some bold steps of his own, and in the end he bought Naomi's land and made Ruth his wife. Though Ruth and Naomi thought their lives would be bitter and difficult, they discovered that God had been working to bring a new joy and hope. God turned their bitterness into blessing.

Session 3: The Unnamed Bleeding Woman: Healing from the Inside Out

MAIN OBJECTIVE

To encourage us to reach out to Jesus when we're weary of waiting, trusting that He is enough.

SCRIPTURE FOCUS

Mark 5:24-34

BIBLE STORY OVERVIEW

This week we learned about the unnamed bleeding woman. This woman had been bleeding for twelve years, and because of this she was considered unclean in her society. However, it does seem that she had money because she had exhausted medical options before she found herself desperately pushing through a crowd to get to Jesus. Jesus was on His way to heal Jairus's daughter when crowds surrounded him, hoping to be healed or at least to get a good look at this healer passing through their town. The unnamed bleeding woman would have had to come out of hiding and push through a gathering she was not invited to in order to get to Jesus. She made it close enough to touch the hem of his robe, and immediately she felt her body be healed from disease. She felt relief. Her desperate faith had made her well with one touch of a coat. Jesus felt power go out from him and scanned the crowd. When they finally met face to face, Jesus spoke a blessing of peace to the woman. Not only did he heal her; he looked at her and spoke to her—a gift that gave her a new outlook on her life, a new sense of belonging, and a peace she had never known before.

Session 4: Martha: Embracing the Better Blessing

MAIN OBJECTIVE

To encourage us to look for God's better blessing, which is and always will be with Him.

SCRIPTURE FOCUS

John 11

BIBLE STORY OVERVIEW

This week we read the story of Lazarus's illness, death, and resurrection, focusing on Mary and Martha's response to the situation. Jesus was good friends with Lazarus and his sisters. If anyone would have an "in" with Jesus, it would be them! But when Jesus received word of Lazarus's illness, he didn't run to them. He took care of some other things and then headed their way. By the time Jesus got there, Lazarus was dead. When Martha and later Mary ran to meet Jesus, their faces were surely wet with tears. They told Jesus that he should have been there, that Lazarus wouldn't be dead if Jesus had come sooner. But Jesus had planned to demonstrate the glory of God and was operating on a different time line. Although Jesus wept at the thought of losing Lazarus—showing us that he can relate to our human emotion—and from his anger at human suffering as a consequence of sin, he absolutely demonstrated divine power when he raised Lazarus to life again.

Notes

Week 1: Hannah

1. Ronald F. Youngblood, *Nelson's Illustrated Bible Dictionary: New and Enhanced Edition* (Nashville, TN: Thomas Nelson, 2014), 917.
2. See Youngblood, *Nelson's Illustrated Bible Dictionary*, 1057.
3. E. Ray Clendenen and Jeremy Royal Howard, eds., *Holman Illustrated Bible Commentary* (Nashville, TN: B&H Publishing Group, 2015), 278.
4. Clendenen and Howard, *Holman Illustrated Bible Commentary*, 278.
5. Names of God, https://www.blueletterbible.org/study/misc/name_god.cfm. Accessed May 26, 2019.
6. David Guzik, Study Guide for 1 Samuel 1, https://www.blueletterbible.org/Comm /guzik_david/StudyGuide2017-1Sa/1Sa-1.cfm?a=237011. Accessed May 26, 2019.
7. Youngblood, *Nelson's Illustrated Bible Dictionary*, 797.
8. Warren W. Wiersbe, *The Wiersbe Bible Commentary, Old Testament* (Colorado Springs, CO; David C. Cook Publisher, 2007), 495.
9. *Shalom*, https://biblehub.com/hebrew/7965.htm. Accessed May 26, 2019.
10. "The Marshmallow Test," https://www.youtube.com/watch?v=QX_oy9614HQ. Accessed February 26, 2019.
11. David Guzik. Accessed May 26, 2019.
12. *Pala*, https://biblehub.com/hebrew/6381.htm, Accessed May 26, 2019.
13. Wiersbe, *Wiersbe Bible Commentary*, 494.

Week 2: Ruth

1. *Moab*, https://www.biblegateway.com/resources/all-women-bible/Naomi. Accessed December 20, 2018.
2. Clendenen and Howard, *Holman Illustrated Bible Commentary*, see page 272.
3. Wiersbe, *Wiersbe Bible Commentary*, 479-480.
4. Wiersbe, *Wiersbe Bible Commentary*, 480.
5. Clendenden and Howard, *Holman Illustrated Bible Commentary*, 272.
6. *The ESV Study Bible* (Wheaton, IL: Crossway, 2008), 479.

7. Wiersbe, *Wiersbe Bible Commentary*, 482.
8. Clendenen and Howard, *Holman Illustrated Bible Commentary*, 274.
9. Wiersbe, *Wiersbe Bible Commentary*, 482.
10. Kinsman-redeemer, https://www.blueletterbible.org/Comm/guzik_david /StudyGuide2017-Rth/Rth-3.cfm?a=235009. Accessed May 27, 2019.
11. Joel B. Green, ed., *The Common English Study Bible* (Nashville, TN: Common English Bible, 2013), 410.
12. Wiersbe, *Wiersbe Bible Commentary*, 486.
13. Acknowledge as a wife, https://biblehub.com/commentaries/barnes/ruth/3.htm. Accessed on January 10, 2019.

Week 3: The Unnamed Bleeding Woman

1. Laura Story and Jennifer Schuchmann, *When God Doesn't Fix It: Lessons You Never Wanted to Learn, Truth You Can't Live Without*. Nashville, TN: W Publishing Group, 2015. 223.
2. Story and Schuchmann, *When God Doesn't Fix It*, 142.
3. Story and Schuchmann, *When God Doesn't Fix It*, 142.
4. Joni Eareckson Tada, *A Place of Healing: Wrestling with the Mysteries of Suffering, Pain, and God's Sovereignty* (Colorado Springs, CO: David C Cook, 2010), 25.
5. *The ESV Study Bible*, 212.
6. Wiersbe, *Wiersbe Bible Commentary*, 224.
7. Clinton E. Arnold, ed., *Zondervan Illustrated Bible Backgrounds Commentary: Volume 1, Matthew, Mark, Luke*. Grand Rapids, Michigan: Zondervan, 2002), 35.
8. Clendenen, *Holman Illustrated Bible Commentary*, 1058.
9. David Guzik, Study Guide for Mark 5, https://www.blueletterbible.org/Comm/guzik _david/StudyGuide2017-Mar/Mar-5.cfm?a=962027. Accessed May 28, 2019.
10. Arnold, *Zondervan, Volume* I, 138.
11. David Guzik, Study Guide for Luke 17, https://www.blueletterbible.org/Comm/guzik _david/StudyGuide2017-Luk/Luk-17.cfm?a=990006. Accessed May 28, 2019.
12. John Ortberg, *The Me I Want to Be: Becoming God's Best Version of You* (Grand Rapids, Michigan: Zondervan, 2010), 72.
13. *Sózó*, https://biblehub.com/greek/4982.htm. Accessed May 28, 2019.
14. *Eiréné*, https://biblehub.com/greek/1515.htm. Accessed May 28, 2019.

Week 4: Martha

1. Youngblood, *Nelson's Illustrated Bible Dictionary*, 681.
2. Clinton E. Arnold, gen. ed., Andreas J. Köstenberger, commentary on John, *Zondervan Illustrated Bible Backgrounds Commentary: Volume 2: John, Acts* (Grand Rapids, MI: Zondervan, 2002), 108.
3. Youngblood, *Nelson's Illustrated Bible Dictionary*, 400.

4.   Youngblood, *Nelson's Illustrated Bible Dictionary*, 708.

5.   Youngblood, *Nelson's Illustrated Bible Dictionary*, 447.

6.   Larry Crabb, *Shattered Dreams: God's Unexpected Pathway to Joy* (Colorado Springs, CO: Waterbrook Press, 2001), 34.

7.   Arnold and Köstenberger, *Zondervan*, Volume 2, 109.

8.   Arnold and Köstenberger, *Zondervan*, Volume 2, 109.

9.   John Piper, https://www.desiringgod.org/embrace-the-life-god-has-given-you. Accessed March 1, 2019.

10. David Guzik, Study Guide for John 11, https://www.blueletterbible.org/Comm/guzik _david/StudyGuide2017-Jhn/Jhn-11.cfm. Accessed May 29, 2019,

11. Tim Keller, https://youtu.be/F_Wkilqwjjo - timestamp 26:33-27:00. Accessed May 29, 2019.

12. Rick Warren Tweet.jpg, #RealComfort, July 13, 2018, 7:57 PM.

13. Arnold and Köstenberger, *Zondervan*, Volume 2, 111.

14. Story and Schuchmann, *When God Doesn't Fix It*, 142.

15. Crabb, *Shattered Dreams*, 82.

16. Janet Holm McHenry, *The Complete Guide to the Prayers of Jesus: What Jesus Prayed and How It Can Change Your Life*. (Grand Rapids, MI: Bethany House, 2018), 70.

17. Tammy Trent, https://tammytrent.com/about/bio Website video 3:23 mark.

18. Tammy Trent with Gwen Smith, https://itunes.apple.com/us/podcast/graceologie -with-gwen-smith/id1393906123?mt=2&i=1000430120123 (47:45 mark).

More Women's Bible Studies from Barb Roose

A Bible Study By
Barbara L. Roose

Beautiful Already

Reclaiming God's Perspective on Beauty

Beautiful Already: Reclaiming God's Perspective on Beauty

Participant Workbook
9781501813542 | $15.99

Leader Guide
9781501813566 | $13.99

Video – DVD
9781501813580 | $49.99

Winning Your Ugly Struggle *with* Beauty

ENOUGH ALREADY

Barbara L. Roose

Bible Study Companion Book

Enough Already: Winning Your Ugly Struggle with Beauty

9781426789014 | $15.99

A leader guide and Video-DVD are available for each Bible study.

Did you enjoy studying *I'm Waiting, God,* or other studies by Barb Roose?
Please share a review on your favorite online retailer site or social media platform.

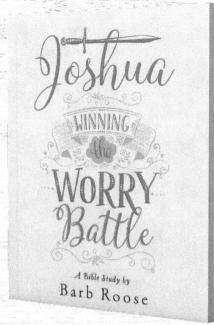

Joshua: *Winning the Worry Battle*

Participant Workbook
9781501813603 | $16.99

Leader Guide
9781501813627 | $14.99

Video – DVD
9781501813641 | $49.99

Bible Study Companion Book

Winning the Worry Battle: Life Lessons from the Book of Joshua

9781501857843 | $16.99

Praise

"Barb Roose gives us not only the reasons for the need to limit worry in our lives but also the practical and spiritual tools we need to do more than postpone worry and actually deal with it for the rest of our lives. I love her focus on the freedom that a life of worrying less can bring to each and every one of us. Highly recommended."
—**Kathi Lipp**, best-selling author of *The Husband Project*, *Clutter Free*, and *Overwhelmed*

"Who doesn't want to win the worry battle? Whether it's our health, finances, or relationships, the mental hamster wheel of worry beckons us to constantly turn things over in our minds. Barb Roose shares valuable insights from the Book of Joshua and helps you apply them in very practical ways."
—**Melissa Spoelstra**, speaker and author of six Bible studies and four books including *Romans: Good News that Changes Everything* and *Dare to Hope: Living Intentionally in an Unstable World*

Printed in the USA
CPSIA information can be obtained
at www.ICGtesting.com
LVHW082024021023
759665LV00016B/3